THE LIBRARY OF HOLOCAUST TESTIMONIES

My Heart in a Suitcase

To Susan
Best wishes
Anne L. Fox
1996

The Library of Holocaust Testimonies

Editors: Antony Polonsky, Martin Gilbert CBE, Aubrey Newman,
Raphael F. Scharf, Ben Helfgott

Under the auspices of the Yad Vashem Committee of the Board of
Deputies of British Jews and the Centre for Holocaust Studies,
University of Leicester

My Lost World by Sara Rosen
From Dachau to Dunkirk by Fred Pelican
Breathe Deeply, My Son by Henry Wermuth
My Private War by Jacob Gerstenfeld-Maltiel
A Cat Called Adolf by Trude Levi
An End to Childhood by Miriam Akavia
A Child Alone by Martha Blend
I Light a Candle by Gena Turgel
My Heart in a Suitcase by Anne L. Fox

My Heart in a Suitcase

ANNE L. FOX

VALLENTINE MITCHELL
LONDON

First published in 1996 in Great Britain by
VALLENTINE MITCHELL & CO. LTD
Newbury House, 900 Eastern Avenue, London IG2 7HH

and in the United States of America by
VALLENTINE MITCHELL
c/o ISBS, 5804 N.E. Hassalo Street, Portland, Oregon 97213–3644

Copyright © 1996 Anne L. Fox

British Library Cataloguing in Publication Data
Fox, Anne L.
  My Heart in a Suitcase. — (Library of
  Holocaust Testimonies)
  I. Title   II. Series
  940.5318
ISBN 0-85303-311-0

Library of Congress Cataloging-in-Publication Data
Fox, Anne L., 1926–
    My heart in a suitcase / Anne L. Fox.
        p.   cm. — (The Library of Holocaust testimonies)
    ISBN 0-85303-311-0 (pbk.)
      1. Fox, Anne L., 1926–   . 2. Jews—Germany—Biography.
3. Refugees, Jewish—Great Britain—Biography. 4. Jews—Germany—
–History—1933–1945.   I. Title.   II. Series.
DS135.G5f563   1996
943'.004924'0092—dc20
[B]   95-38174
                                                                                            CIP

Cover illustration by Rafal Olbinski

Typeset by Regent Typesetting, London
Printed and bound in Great Britain by
Watkiss Studios, Biggleswade, Beds.

*I dedicate this book to the memory
of my parents.*

Contents

List of Illustrations

Introduction

I always loved to write, but I was not prepared for the difficult process that it takes to evoke memories, especially the painful ones. But I discovered that intense concentration makes it possible to recall forgotten hurts. Feelings resurface, images reappear and events long past become visible in your mind's eye as though they happened yesterday.

The pictures I have included should enable the reader to visualize the world in which I lived, and provide images of the people who were a part of my life. The poems, letters and drawings that had been tucked away in drawers and shoeboxes, have reinforced my recollections. My parents' letters that were saved by my brother without my knowledge and did not come to light until his death, are a personal treasure. Fortunately I took possession of these some time later from my nephew in California. It took another year before I found myself able to decipher them carefully and put them into chronological order. None of them were dated, having been enclosed in other people's correspondence. The insight I gleaned from their writings proved invaluable. I was at last able to see my dear parents in a different light, no longer worshipping them as a love-deprived child, but seeing them as an adult.

I hope that my children, grandchildren, niece and nephews will gain a greater understanding of their mother, grandmother and aunt by reading this book and will appreciate their Jewish heritage.

Here in America, I am called a survivor, a term I do not feel completely comfortable with, but I have used this title whenever I introduce groups to the Holocaust. It is very important to me to talk and lecture on that subject especially to younger children.

I have made my peace with the past. Life has compensated me for my lost childhood by giving me a wonderful husband for the past 50 years and thoughtful and caring children who are raising my four adorable granddaughters with love and concern.

I wish to thank the following for their help and cooperation:

My husband Frank, who encouraged me and proved invaluable as a critic and editor.

My son, Julian, the computer expert.

My good friend, Amelia Gigliotti, who put my hand-scribbled manuscript into her computer.

My daughter, Nina as well as all my friends who encouraged and supported my efforts.

Rafal Olbinski, whose moving artwork graces the cover of this book, and last but not least

Cherie Smith, the moving force in my venture who convinced me that I had a story to tell.

MUTTI'S POEM

In eine Zeit hinein geboren,
Wo Menschentum, Kultur verloren,
Wo Misgunst, Hass, Gewalt vor Recht
Droht zu vernichten ein altes Geschlecht,
Da heisst es fest auf den Füssen stehn,
Und gläubig hoffend nach oben sehn.
Dir gab Gott Verstand, die Seele, das Herz,
Verliere sie nicht in all deinem Schmerz.
Bleib' hilfreich und gut, so schwer es auch ist,
Bekenn' es stolz, dass du Jude bist!

Born into difficult times
Where humanity and culture are lost,
Where ill-will and hatred, power replacing justice,
Threaten to destroy an ancient people,
It is important to take a firm stand
And to look to the heavens with faith.
God gave you understanding, soul, and heart.
Don't ever lose it in all your sorrow.
Remain helpful and kind, however difficult it may be.
Proudly admit that you are a Jew.

(Reconstructed from Memory)

1 • Childhood

The waters of the English Channel swirled behind the ocean liner as she sailed out of Southampton. I was leaving England for a new life in America. By a strange coincidence, the SS *Washington* was the same liner that had brought me to England in 1938, almost eight years earlier. It was hard to recognize the luxury liner of the prewar Hamburg–America Line which had been converted into a troopship during the war.

My thoughts wandered back to my first trip, to my home and family. I could still picture them, my father releasing my mother's arm with his only hand in order to let his clean white handkerchief flutter. My mother, her worn fur coat wrapped tightly around her, her hat pulled down over her forehead to hide her anguish, waving to me, the departing child, their hope and joy.

I did not see their pain as the train pulled out of the station to take me to Hamburg and to the ship that was to carry me across the Channel to England.

Nachkömmling

I was born in Berlin. My mother, Marta, was 38 at the time and my father, Eugen, 43. In the 1920s, 38 was thought of as late for childbearing, and I was considered a *Nachkömmling* (a late child). They named me Annemarie, which was affectionately shortened to Annemie, Miechen, Mielein, and Mie. My brother, Günter, who was already nine years old

1

when I was born was very disappointed with me. What good was this baby that could neither walk nor talk?

Everyone who remembered me as a small child told me that I was chubby. To the often posed question, *'Wovon bist du denn so dick?'* ('What makes you so chubby?'), I would reply, *'Von Tsokolade'*, from eating *Schokolade* (chocolate).

Apparently, I had an early urge to be independent, because I was often reminded that I rejected assistance with just one emphatic expression: *'aneine'* (*'aleine'* –'by myself').

My father had fought for the 'Fatherland' in the First World War, and had lost his left arm on a battlefield in France. Times were difficult after the defeat of 1918 and the German people lived through a period of devastating inflation.

It was not until the twenties that he secured a prominent position with an international bank in Berlin, and our family was comfortably provided for. We employed a maid who slept in a small, narrow room in the apartment, and we were able to afford family vacations at the seaside.

I think back with nostalgia to a stay in Norderney, a resort on the North Sea, where we spent a few weeks in the summer of 1927, my parents, Günter and I, as well as Günter's best friend, Hans. The many photos I have of the holiday show my father in white flannels, my mother wearing a stylish long-waisted loose dress with a white beret, and the three children building sand-castles. I was also photographed in the altogether, playing with a beach ball bigger than I was!

Our apartment in Berlin was on Windscheidstrasse, on the corner of Pestalozzistrasse in Charlottenburg, a western section of the city. The building had eight apartments, two on each floor. There were two stores at street level. Mr Josefsohn had a printing shop on the corner; the other store changed hands several times.

The concierge, as was customary, lived on the ground floor and a gentile family occupied one side of the second floor. Opposite them lived a Jewish couple with a grown son. Their name was Hartwig. We shared the third floor with the Jablonskis. The fourth-floor tenants changed often, and were not part of my life.

Above that floor, the carpeted steps changed to plain wooden ones which led to the attic, where one could boil clothes in a huge copper kettle and hang them up to dry on long lines strung from the rafters.

Windscheidstrasse was a broad street, and the sidewalks were lined with carefully squared-off patches of grass enclosed behind low iron railings. Trees were planted at exact intervals. It was *verboten* to step on the grass, but we children balanced merrily on the railings and used the broad sidewalks for our hoops and hopscotch games for skipping, rope jumping, and – of course – tricycling and scooter riding.

My brother and I used to walk up to the third floor, along the broad carpeted staircase. There was also an elevator but we were not allowed to use it as children.

The door of the apartment opened into a small vestibule furnished with a table and chairs facing a *Vitrine* (curio cabinet) where my father's Iron Cross was prominently displayed. Two doors opened onto this foyer, the kitchen, with a backdoor going to the rear balcony, and a medium sized front room, which was occupied by my grandmother and later a lodger. The long, narrow corridor, from which the other rooms led off, was separated by a curtain. My parents' bedroom situated at the very end of this long dark hallway was a large airy room with big double windows. It still contained a white *Kachelofen* (tiled oven), no longer in use since we had central heating throughout the building.

My parents slept in large adjoining twin beds topped with plump pillows and the ever present *Federbett* (feather quilt). I was only allowed to sleep there when I was sick. My crib and *Wickeltisch* (changing table) were also in this room until I was big enough to be moved into another room. The room also contained a large marble-topped dresser with a mirror. The bowl and pitcher set which stood there was used regularly in the mornings by my father, who rather scorned the bathroom with its running water, basin and bathtub.

It was in the bedroom that I first became aware of my father's affliction. His left arm was only a stump. It had been amputated at the elbow. Later I learned that he had been shot through the elbow in the First World War, while serving as a German soldier in France. During the day, he wore a cumbersome prosthesis made of metal and wood which was strapped around his shoulders. The only thing protruding from his jacket was a brown-gloved hand. With the aid of a button on the side of the thumb, he was able to open and close this hand. Since I was born after the war, I accepted my father's deformity quite naturally.

The household revolved around *Vati*, as we called him. Although he was of medium height and of delicate build, he stood tall and straight. The photograph in his army uniform shows him self-confident and handsome. He was a quiet, serious man, not given to frivolous talk. An avid reader, he owned a large library of books and acquainted me with the fairy tales of Hans Christian Andersen, the favourite stories of his youth. He possessed many volumes, all handsomely bound in yellow leather.

My mother waited on him hand and foot and brought all his meals and snacks to him in the dining room or on the balcony, knowing that his remaining hand was very unsteady. She affectionately called him *Euchen*. Eugen was his given name.

Mother, or *Mutti*, was always a source of comfort and love. She liked to laugh and joke, and she was popular with the shopkeepers and salespeople. By profession, she was a photographer and had worked at a studio in Berlin, photographing portraits of individuals and groups. This was very unusual for a woman in the early 1900s. It was more customary for women to stay at home. She must have enjoyed

1 Vati in the German Army

2 Marta /Berthold /Edith /Elsa

her work, because she converted the bathroom into a dark-room and brought her work home. On many occasions a red bulb would be glowing over the washbasin and glass plates resting in the bathtub. Her camera was a big black box on spindly folding legs. It was covered with a black cloth, under which she would creep to focus, while her hand held up the crucial rubber ball that she squeezed to activate the lens. Due to her skill, I have many good photographs in my possession.

Mutti was born in Celle, a small town near Hanover. She was one of four children – three girls: Else, Marta, and Edith and one boy, Berthold. My mother, Marta, was the middle one, and (to me) the prettiest.

Else, five years her senior, was rather serious and seemed old before her time. We used to visit her family in a cluttered apartment in Neukölln, in the south-eastern district of Berlin, where she lived with her husband, Julius (or Jule), and her daughter, Karla. Else's hair was completely white when I was small, which made her look more like my grandmother than my aunt. She worked in a large office, supervising several typists.

Karla was almost 18 years my senior. She was petite, with strikingly dark hair and dark brown eyes. Tante Else and Karla visited us often. Due to financial difficulties, Karla was not able to pursue an academic career, and worked as a sales-girl at Hermann Tietz, a large department store. She hoped to work her way up to management. However, her ambitions were thwarted in 1933 when she was laid off. Although this was a Jewish firm, non-Aryan employees were slowly being weeded out. She cried bitterly about her lost job. Not long after her dismissal, she met a handsome young man named Paul at 'Krumme Lanke', a popular beer hall, where young people gathered to dance and drink. It was love at first sight! As Paul was a gentile, and the Nuremberg laws of 1935 pro-hibited mixed marriages, marriage was out of the question.

Paul was strongly opposed to the rising Nazi regime. He refused to give the customary salute: *'Heil Hitler'* at the dental laboratory where he worked and his employer advised him to leave the country. The latter had tried to move his business to Addis Ababa, but that had failed. Paul scanned the dental journals for help wanted abroad and sent out applications for a job as a technician. Always a ladies' man, he persuaded a young woman in charge of distributing the dental magazines to let him see the advertising page before the journal was sent out, so that he had an advantage over other applicants also looking for positions. He was lucky and obtained a job in Argentina and a ticket to Buenos Aires.

Once Paul was established in Argentina, he found a room at the house of a refugee woman and saved his money to bring Karla over. When she finally received the money, she tried to buy a ticket, only to be told that the steamship company issued only round-trip fares. In vain, she tried to explain that she only needed a one-way ticket, but the company refused. She didn't have enough money to pay the full fare. As she sat on a bench crying, a gentleman approached. When he heard her story, he miraculously produced a ticket for her. It was a time both of unaccountable good luck and unaccountable bad luck!

Karla and Paul were married in a civil ceremony in Argentina. Soon after the wedding, Karla went to work to put aside money to bring her parents out of Germany. They came in 1938 and moved into the apartment with the young couple.

Edith, my mother's youngest sister, was plump, pretty and talkative, a complete contrast to her oldest sister. I liked to visit their home in Birkenwerder in a northern suburb of Berlin. Her husband, Max, owned a haberdashery, and they lived above the store. Max was a big man, solidly built with a lusty voice and a mouthful of gold teeth. Everything about him was oversized: his shoulders, his head, his hands and his feet. He towered over Aunt Edith. I loved to go into the store and rummage amongst the socks, underwear, hats, suspenders, aprons, nightdresses, and work clothes. They had one child, Fred-Paul, or *Pumpel* as he was called, because he was roly-poly. He did not suffer me kindly; I was not in his league since he was a budding architect. At the age of 14 he spent his time building elaborate edifices with small blocks, complete with towers and gates, using anything he could find like spools, lids and screwtops to crown these structures.

The family owned a large German Shepherd dog named 'Asta' whom I loved. We used to throw eggshells out of the upstairs kitchen window, which Asta caught gleefully and crushed with her strong teeth. They also had a car, which to me was quite a luxury. Whenever I spent a weekend with Uncle Max and Aunt Edith, we would take a ride into the countryside, stopping at every village church which Fred-Paul sketched in detail. I marvelled at his talent.

At this time, Max's father lived with them, a man in his 80s. He kept us children amused with his stories while the adults worked in the store. Some of his tales were about Frederick the Great, *Der Alte Fritz*, who had been a most colourful character. He was beloved by his people as an enlightened ruler and, when time allowed, he played the flute and composed. The tale that remains in my mind was about the row of buttons on the soldiers' uniforms which ran up the sleeves from the wrist to the elbow. As the story goes, *Der Alte Fritz* caught one of his soldiers wiping his nose on the back of his sleeve, whereupon he ordered that buttons should be sewn on.

My own grandfather, Simon, died in 1909. He had been a merchant in Celle, where he settled in the late 1800s. My grandmother or 'Omi', whose given name was Balbina, or *Bienchen*, was born in Zinten, East Prussia. I can only assume that she met her husband nearby. They moved to Berlin in the early 1900s, where the youngest child – a son, Berthold – was born.

3 Opa Simon Jachmann

4 Omi Balbina (Blenchen) Jachmann

Omi lived in a cluttered apartment on the other side of Berlin, the Eastern part – not far from Aunt Else. Later, in the mid-1930s, she came to live with us, bringing a few pieces of her own furniture. She moved into the front room off the entrance hall. All day long she busied herself sewing, mainly for me. I dreaded the fittings because of her remarks about 'the little puddings', making me feel very self-conscious about my budding womanhood. For her 75th birthday, my parents threw a large party, and all the relatives came. I provided the entertainment by dancing in a fancy costume, which I had put together myself out of crepe paper. She died in 1937, a few months after the family party.

My father's family consisted of four sisters, only one of whom ever married. This sister, Lilli, left Germany in 1933 for Yugoslavia with her husband, and severed all ties with the family. The other three, Grete, Erna, and Trude, lived together in a dark apartment in the Sybelstrasse in Berlin. It was disagreeable for me to have to visit them. I felt uncomfortable and confined. The rooms smelled of stale cooking, and the hallways were dark and dusty. Besides, I disliked the smothering attention they showered on me, their only niece. It was unpleasant to be touched and kissed by them, especially by Erna, who was short and plump with reddish blonde hair. Her heavy bosom acted as a bumper when she pulled me towards her. Grete was also short, but not heavy. She wore a black ribbon around her neck to hide a goitre. Her hair was dark and very straight, just like mine. How I longed to have curls!

Both Erna and Grete were constantly fussing over me. Trude had more appeal for me than the others. She was taller, better looking, and had more understanding for my feelings. Whenever they came to visit us, I disappeared very discreetly under a table or simply escaped to the neighbours, to avoid being kissed and fondled by them all.

My father supported his sisters financially as best he could,

5 Omi's 75th Birthday

6 Günter and I, 1928

but I know there were many arguments, especially with Erna, who was more abrasive than the others. They were a constant worry to him. I never knew my paternal grandparents, nor did my father ever mention them to me. The only members of his family familiar to me were a man and a woman portrayed on two paintings, which hung in ornate gold frames on the wall of the library. They were painted at some time in the 1800s. I did not know their names, nor did I ever ask for them. The man sat proudly upright, his regular features framed by dark hair and sideburns. He wore a velvet waistcoat and large bow-tie, with a gold watch-chain dangling on his chest. His ruffled shirtsleeves fell over his hands, one of which was gracefully resting on the chair, the other by his side.

His wife wore a lace cap and her dress, also trimmed with lace, was draped over her tight corset. At her neck she had a brooch with the pictures of two children on it, a boy and a girl. Were they her children? I'm afraid I'll never know, but I like to think that they were. The brooch survived. It is in my possession, and I wear it with nostalgia. I was told that it was passed along to the girls in the family, and my daughter will inherit it.

My ancestors must have been prominent people who could commission an artist to paint them. By their dress and proud bearing, I judged them to be educated people of importance in the community where they lived, presumably Gumbinnen, East Prussia, since that was my father's birthplace.

Vati's family moved to Berlin where he received a very good education. He attended the *'Französische Gymnasium'*, a very prestigious boys school. I can only assume that he also received an extensive Jewish education, because he read Hebrew well and knew the prayers. Although he attended the Synagogue on the High Holy days at the Reform Temple, our family was assimilated and did not adhere to most of the Jewish laws. We did not keep the Sabbath, nor did we keep a kosher house. Since my father was good at mathematics, he

7 The Young Couple

eventually entered the field of finance and banking. He met my mother a year or so before they married in 1913. It must have been a civil ceremony, because I never came across a picture of my mother dressed as a bride. There does exist a lovely portrait of the handsome young couple.

Mutti looked slender and lithe, in an embroidered dress topped by a short-sleeved jacket, her gaze with just a hint of a smile, the heavy dark hair framing her face, a thick braid wound over her ears like huge snails, or *Schnecken* as they used to call this hair style. Around her neck she wears a delicate necklace with a diamond pendant. This piece of jewellery also miraculously survived and is in my possession. Vati leans toward her. He is dressed in a cutaway jacket with a vest and striped trousers, a shirt with a starched stand-up collar *Vatermörder* (father killer), a patterned wide tie, and a handkerchief in his left breast pocket. He sports a brush-like moustache and wears a *pince-nez*, so fashionable at the time. He is quite impressive, with his high forehead and slightly receding hairline. There is just a shadow of a smile on his face, as on mother's. It is reflected in their eyes. Both are seated on velvet cushions.

The people who were closest to me and my parents were the Jablonskis. They lived in the next-door apartment, the back doors of which led to a common balcony overlooking the backyard of the apartment house. There was a square of grass in the centre, surrounded by a walkway. To the side was a large wooden structure meant to hold the rugs which the housewives or maids brought down to beat with bamboo carpet beaters until the thick clouds of dust had dissipated. The entertainers would come into this yard – a string of singers, organ-grinders with or without monkeys, instrumentalists, all sorts of people who were hoping for a few coins. I would beg the adults for some money, wrap it up tightly in paper, and throw it over the balcony railing, aiming as close to the entertainers as I could get!

This same balcony was my passageway to escape and indulgence. I adored 'Tante Käthe and Onkel Richard', our neighbours. To them I was the child they never had. Although Onkel Richard was the father of twins from a previous marriage, Olga and Theo – both redheads – they were by that time adult and independent. Theo emigrated to New York in the early 30s, and Olga was not often at home.

Tante Käthe was a round, petite woman with a lovely face. Everything about her was soft, her features, her hair, her body, her voice, even her clothes. I buried myself in her gently yielding bosom. Onkel Richard, by contrast, was a tall stately man, who towered above her. His hair was fuzzy and grey. He was probably in his sixties. His grey moustache – which he wore in the style of Kaiser Wilhelm II – waxed and twirled upward at the ends – was very impressive.

16

8 Uncle Richard
and Aunt Käthe

Every Sunday morning, Onkel Richard took his violin
out of its case in anticipation of the teacher who would come
to give him a lesson and to accompany his playing on
the grand piano in their beautiful music room. All I ever
remember hearing him play was Boccherini's Minuet. At
least, that is the only piece of music that ingrained itself in my
memory.

The Jablonskis cuddled and spoiled me, consoled me when
I was unhappy, and fed me when I did not like the food at
home. Onkel Richard would sit me on his knee and make
drawings for me or show me how to solve crossword puzzles,
while Aunt Käthe supplied me with beads, ribbons and laces
for my dolls. She very cleverly made up sewing sets which I

17

gave to girl-friends as birthday gifts. I confided all my secret desires to her and happily accepted the expensive dresses she bought for me. Their apartment became my refuge and safe harbour. I made myself a den under a round table in their library, where the heavy table cover reached to the floor and hid me from view.

The Jablonskis emigrated to America in the spring of 1938, and I felt very upset to see their apartment stripped bare and cluttered with boxes, trunks, and crates. It was a sad good-bye, but to a child, America is not that far and nothing is forever.

Clouds Gather

My father's income had diminished since 1933 when he was forced to resign his job at the International Bank. By Nazi decree, no Jews were allowed to work in that capacity. It took him a few months to find employment as a clerk in the offices of a Jewish organization – quite a come-down for a proud man. Vati was visibly crushed by the loss of his prestigious job. The wrinkles deepened on his face, and he wore a constant expression of worry. Mutti guarded his privacy by keeping us children in the kitchen with her. On Sundays, he would ask me to go with him on long walks. I always balked at that and had to be bribed and coerced into accompanying him. It took all of Mutti's gentle persuasion to convince me that Vati really wanted my company. I found it difficult to keep up with him, as he walked vigorously, tapping the pavement with his silver-topped cane.

One incident involving my father stands out clearly in my mind. Having come home from playing in the sandbox one day, my mother urged me to show my father how dirty my hands were, and told me to say, 'Look at my clean hands.' I did this, thinking it was a great joke, whereupon he slapped my face. Crying, I ran back to my mother for comfort. How badly she must have felt! She had anticipated his amusement at the 'joke', instead, he must have resented the interruption of his work with something so trivial.

I must have been five or six years old at the time of this incident. It was a devastating experience which puzzled me for many years, until – as an adult – I realized that it was the time of Hitler's fast rise to power. In this year, 1932, the year before he was appointed *Reichskanzler*, my father must have had premonitions of his family's crumbling future. Besides, not being a man given to laughter and jokes, he had no time for childish pranks.

During these years of rising anti-Semitism, my maternal grandmother, Omi, came to live with us until her death in 1937. She occupied the front room which was subsequently rented out. The furniture was removed, and it then contained a single bed, a desk, a wardrobe, a table and chairs. Mother found a tenant, a single gentleman by the name of Rudi Müller. This amiable, rotund, good-natured man, with his pronounced Saxon accent, became affectionately known as 'Müllerchen'.

He was also a source of endless 'goodies', since he was employed by Stollwerk, one of the largest chocolate manufacturers in Germany at the time. Damaged lots, broken Easter eggs, and leftover Christmas candy found their way into our closet, and after dinner I would help myself to some of these treasures. My mother was very fond of Müllerchen, and would spend many evenings in his room, talking and listening to Spanish records. He loved Spanish music and often visited Barcelona, his favourite city. Müllerchen stayed with us until a few days before the infamous *Kristallnacht* (Night of Crystal). He was not Jewish, and knowing of the brutality and power of the Nazis, he feared recrimination for living in a Jewish home and was concerned for his safety. However, he continued to visit my parents. Much later I learned from my brother that Müller met a sad end. He hid in a cellar at the time of Berlin's occupation by Russian forces, and was shot.

Müllerchen was not the only *Untermieter* (tenant) we had. As my parents' finances declined, they were forced to rent out our elegant sitting room, the Green Salon, which had been designed and decorated by J.R. Davidson, an architect married to mother's best friend. This room had dark green walls accented with gold, and the furniture was painted green and upholstered with the same shade of velvet. There was an elaborate chandelier and sconces to match, and the architect's framed sketch hung on the wall.

The room was rented to a young lady who was qualifying as a physical education instructor. Every evening we would hear her vault over our lovely green sofa before she turned in for the night. We didn't see much of her. She ate her meals out and only used the room for exercise and sleeping.

Father's study now became Günter's room, and I moved into the tiny, narrow back room that had been his. I didn't mind at all. I spread out my belongings. The many stuffed animals I owned sat on the bed and slept with me at night. My school desk bordered an area reserved for a dolls' corner. I also found space for my wind-up gramophone which Günter had generously bequeathed to me. I played records of the *Schlager* (popular songs) of the period and my favourite record was Paul Robeson singing 'Ol' Man River'.

My dresser was loaded with knick-knacks I had appropriated from Omi, Tante Käthe, and the *Vitrine*, amongst them a blue Wedgwood plate with white angels, glass-blown animals, and china figurines. There were bars on the window, as the room looked out onto the back balcony. It never bothered me – I felt free in my small environment.

Vati must have resented giving up his study with its solid oak desk and wall-to-wall bookcases to Günter, who – as a young adult – needed space to entertain his friends. He used to invite Hans, his best friend from childhood and a few others, including Bobby, whom I considered the best looking. I had a serious crush on him. On occasion, I would listen to the laughter and music filtering through the tightly closed doors, and it aroused my curiosity. Mutti sometimes joined the group, especially when Günter was cutting yellow transparent gelatin disks in order to copy precious records or record the voices of those present. One day, my best friend Dorit and I dressed in my mother's clothes, as eleven-year-olds are inclined to do, borrowed her lipstick and powder as well as jewellery, and crashed Günter's party. Of course, he was mortified, and we were sternly ordered out.

Until 1934, Günter had attended a prestigious *Gymnasium* (boys' high school), but he was unable to complete his schooling because, as a Jew, he was no longer allowed to attend the Kaiser-Friedrich Real Gymnasium. At the age of 17 he was forced to look for employment. Boys at that age became apprentices in offices or to tradesmen. Günter became a 'gofer' in a textile firm. He hated his job but was aware that he had to make at least a small contribution to the household, as the financial situation became more and more precarious. Vati's face showed his worry and concern about supporting his family as well as contributing to the upkeep of his three unmarried sisters on his clerk's wages.

Günter and I spent a lot of time in the kitchen with my mother. The kitchen, with its mottled black and white stone floor, was spacious and comfortable. Mutti cooked on a gas burner that had been placed on top of a large built-in wood stove, long out of use. Next to it was a big oven bearing the name Lucullus. After many years, I figured out that it was named after the Roman general and statesman who was known for his elaborate feasts. The large square wooden table in the middle of the room was only used for meals by us children. Our main meal was served in the dining room.

Vati enjoyed a bottle of malt beer with his meals, and Mutti had a small barrel of beer delivered every week or ten days by a man with a horse-drawn wagon. She carefully funnelled the liquid into blue, green or brown bottles, added water, and closed them tightly with the attached rubber-lined cap. Before she took a bottle to Vati, she placed a looped hose around it and attached it to the cold water tap to let the running water cool the beer.

We did not have a refrigerator. Perishables were stored in the pantry, an area as big as a large closet, lined with shelves. One year, Günter and I pooled our money and bought Mutti a small ice-box for her birthday. We had to purchase large blocks of ice from the men with heavy aprons and big tongs, who came around the neighbourhood in horse-drawn ice wagons.

Mutti was always busy. When we could no longer afford a maid, she cooked, shopped, cleaned the apartment and saw to our needs. She was also the peacemaker who smoothed over little quarrels which erupted between father and Günter. Vati shared very few of his thoughts and concerns with us apart from his love of music. Before losing his arm in the war, he had played the violin. One day, he retrieved the instrument from under the divan in the study and handed it to me with these words:

'Take it to school and give it to your music teacher. He will find a deserving student to give it to.' I was crushed. I wanted to play it but did not have the presence of mind to voice my wish at the time. Later, I regretted not speaking up.

My own love of music was stimulated by the pianola in our living-room. The size and shape of an ordinary upright, the glass window above the keyboard betrayed the mechanism with its dots and dashes that converted the perforations on the paper rolls to sounds as they passed over the metal rollers. The rolls were neatly labelled and stacked in the space below the keyboard. All one had to do was extend one's hands over the stiff keys, put one's feet on the pedals, turn on the motor, and 'voila'! one became an accomplished pianist.

Taking the rolls from their carefully labelled boxes, Günter introduced me to the classics: Wagner, Puccini, Rossini, Dvořák, Brahms, and many more. My favourites were Dvořák's 'Slavonic Dances' and Brahms' 'Hungarian Dances'. Günter would sit at the piano using the hand and foot controls, pretending he was the virtuoso producing all that wonderful music, while I danced.

My brother loved live music and went to many concerts. He knew the artists by name and carefully copied the programmes and names of performers into a book in beautiful calligraphy. Günter was also the one who introduced me to opera, namely *Christ Elflein*, a Christmas story for children. The title role was sung by Erna Berger, his idol. Soon after that, he took me to *Hänsel und Gretel*. I enjoyed it, but I never became the opera buff he was.

As we could no longer afford either a live-in maid or seashore vacations after my father lost his position in the bank, I was sent to a Jewish children's camp in the summer of 1935. I hated it passionately. We had to sleep in large dormitories, were herded like cattle and ate at long tables in a big dining hall. I promptly started to throw up at every meal, and was consequently separated from the others and seated at a small table by myself. My condition was ascribed to heat stroke. I fared better the following year, when I was sent to another Jewish *Kinderheim* near the Baltic Sea. We bathed in *Sole*, mineral water with a strong odour of sulphur and the colour of brown swamp. We were also taken to the beaches, where we frantically searched for amber. Every little chip was treasured, but the luckiest find was a piece in which an insect had become embedded.

The constantly worsening political situation in Germany took its toll on my worried parents, but being a child, I was protected and shielded. In 1936, I had to leave the public elementary school in the Witzlebenstrasse where I was a pupil. I had not felt any anti-Semitism directed against me. I

23

had participated in all the activities of my class, even when we were marched to a nearby thoroughfare to line the sidewalks in order to cheer Hitler who was passing by with a lengthy motorcade. I am sure I also raised my arm in the Hitler salute. Once we were taken out of class to greet Mussolini, '*Il Duce*' and I must have yelled for him, too.

The marching Brownshirts, with their hobnail boots and swastika flags, became a common sight. We tried to ignore them and drew back into our apartment, closing the windows. My little friend, Tucke, who lived on the second floor, became reluctant to come up to play, and my mother probably felt uneasy if I went to her flat where I had often gone to play with her brother's castle and toy soldiers. Her older brother, Hans, was often seen in his brown shirt and black kerchief, a black belt across his chest and a swastika on his armband. The father was one of the first to wear the black uniform and boots of the S.S.

My parents avoided the family, which was not so easy, since they lived just one flight up and rarely used the elevator. Mutti may have greeted them with a cheery '*Guten Tag*', but my father must have averted his face and looked the other way when they met. The boys were amongst the marchers whose heavy boots clanked on the cobblestone streets, as they waved their swastika flags and gleefully sang:

> *Wenn Judenblut vom Messer spritzt*
> *Dann geht's nochmal so gut!*
> (When Jewish blood spurts from the knife
> Everything will be much better!)

I didn't mind losing Tucke's friendship since she was a few years younger than me. My best friends were Dorit and Renate. In those days in Berlin in the thirties, *Anbobeln* (dressing up) was our favourite game. We played it in utmost privacy, generally at my home, since it afforded the most space and least adult interference. Our 'props' were stored in an oversized cardboard box which had found a place on top of a linen wardrobe in the long hallway of our large apartment. The box contained mainly old lace curtains, my mother's worn petticoats and discarded dresses, outdated hats, shunned jewellery and ribbons, and Dorit's favourite, a filmy green scarf dotted with beads like dewdrops. There was a peasant costume consisting of a long red skirt, a lace blouse with puffy sleeves, an apron, a velvet hat with a huge plaid bow and long ribbons, and last, but not least, a gold ribbon-trimmed *Mieder* (bodice) which was laced up around gold buttons.

One day, when Renate – portraying an angel – was wearing this costume, one of the buttons came off the Mieder and hit the floor. *'Engel, du hast deinen Knopf verloren'* ('Angel, you lost your button'), proclaimed Dorit, breaking the thread of illusion and make-believe that we had woven. We cracked up with giggles and retrieved the wayward button.

Another item we cherished in this box was a braid of my mother's thick, reddish-brown hair, wrapped in tissue paper, which in turn perched on Renate's blond head or extended Dorit's or my brown hair. Aided by these props and our vivid imaginations, we invented endless stories of poor orphans found by kings and princesses, waifs rescued by angels, siblings parted by evil and reunited by miracles. It was a tireless game, especially for dreary wet or cold afternoons when we were not chased out of the house for fresh air.

Some of the plays we presented were based on the stories and poems we found in a series of anthologies called *Auerbach's Kinderkalender* (Auerbach's Children's Calendar). I had many of these red bound volumes, which were our favourite reading along with Else Uri's extensive tales of *Nesthäkchen* (Fledgling). This prolific writer of children's books managed to write one volume about every stage of a girl's life, from toddler to grandmother. I had the privilege of

9 Mutti wearing the Costume we used for Dressing-up

meeting the author, a lovely little white-haired lady, since she was an aunt of my Uncle Berthold's wife. I vividly recall her large apartment, her friendly smile, and also that she gave me a book which must have been an author's copy, as it had many pencil notations in it. Else Uri's books were adored by all the girls of our generation.

Dorit, Renate and I utilized our long hallway for acrobatics as well as dance space, pretending to be ballerinas. For performances, we dressed in knickers and vests, which were tied with ribbons as was our hair. One of us wore white, one blue and one pink.

Renate was the least imaginative of us ten- to eleven-year-olds. Her mother was a seamstress and worked at home. I never met her father. I believe her parents were divorced. Renate lived about three blocks away in a small apartment with her mother and brother. We rarely played there. It seemed that she was always glad to get away and play at our apartment or Dorit's.

Dorit, whimsical, lively, prone to giggles, was close to me. To Dorit I became 'Micke', a name she chose because I was enamoured of Mickey Mouse after seeing the Disney character in a film. I entertained my friends by putting both hands on my head, bending my knees, and squeaking.

Dorit was an only child of older parents and we exchanged visits frequently. The family lived only two short blocks away from us in the *Hinterhaus* (rear building) of two dingy brown apartment houses separated by a courtyard. That courtyard, on occasions, became a graveyard for dead birds that we found. We gave them a decent burial in a cigar box and marked the grave with sticks. Of course, the service was non-denominational, since Dorit was Protestant.

Religion was never an issue in our friendship. Renate was also a Christian, but neither of the girls came from churchgoing families. The fact that we shared our religious holidays was of great importance to me. I think back to the small, but colourful Christmas tree in Dorit's apartment, and the goodies we packed into a doll's suitcase to share on our sledding outings in the nearby Lietzensee Park. By the same token, Dorit lit Chanukah candles with us and tasted Matzo and Charoset (chopped apples with nuts) at Passover. Herr Sasse, her father – supported by a sturdy walking stick – often accompanied us on outings, and took us to his small garden plot, a kind of victory garden outside Berlin, which we reached by train and walking. That was the closest I came to gardening since our family was limited to window boxes on our balconies. Ours sprouted nothing but 'ice flowers', which bore purple blooms in the late summer.

At Christmas time Herr Sasse would take us to the outdoor Christmas market that was set up yearly on one of the larger streets nearby. There were rows of stalls with toys, crafts, decorations, and foods, a child's delight, especially when we had some change in our pockets. When it snowed, the vendors in their booths bundled up right to their red noses and stamped their feet to keep warm.

We never minded the cold. It was dry, but not penetrating. Dorit and I went skating on the lake at Lietzensee Park, which was open to the public as soon as the ice was thick enough to be safe. You could stay all day for ten *Pfennig*! For about the same amount of pennies you could buy hot chocolate in the little shack where we fastened our skates to our shoes with a key that dangled by a string around our neck. Only really good skaters had boots with skates attached, and were the envy of everyone.

The park with its lake and sledding slopes was the centre of our activities. In the summer, we played ball, climbed the various statues, rolled hoops, rode scooters, fed ducks and swans, and sailed boats in a basin meant for that purpose. In the autumn, we gathered large bagfuls of acorns and horse chestnuts. How silky the chestnuts felt just after we had freed them from their prickly shells! Some of them we strung on

10 The Three Graces: Renate, Dorit and I

chains, carved into baskets or stuck together with toothpicks to make little men or animals.

Dorit and I often went to the movies together, especially to see the Shirley Temple films we adored. The voices of the movie stars were all dubbed, and we were able to sing the songs they featured in German. Both of us were avid collectors of Shirley Temple postcards and the smaller 'glossies' that were sold in packages of ten. We stuck them in albums and admired them.

We would often roam the streets: Pestalozzistrasse, Fritsche-strasse, Kantstrasse, and especially Wilmersdorferstrasse, where the department stores were located. There were the two shoe stores: Leiser and Stiller. These names always amused us, since they both meant 'quieter'. We also shopped for cutoff crusts or day-old cakes at the local bakery. A large bag cost only a few pennies and lasted our whole trip. Or we spent hours picking penny candies from a huge selection of jars. We explored Tietz, the main department store in Charlottenburg, never to make a purchase but to select what we would really like our parents or relatives to buy us for the next birthday. I picked out a large celluloid doll with big blue glass eyes, and I told the saleslady that my Aunt Käthe was going to buy her for my birthday. When Aunt Käthe went to the store to purchase this doll, the saleslady refused to sell her, stating that a little girl had asked her to hold her for her Aunt Käthe, who was going to pick her up. Aunt Käthe laughed and identified herself and was then allowed to purchase the doll. I promptly named her my 'Kätie-doll'.

Nazis in Power

Conditions worsened noticeably for the Jews living in Germany. By 1936 many Jews had departed for nearby European countries that would admit them, and many others opted to abandon their properties and businesses in order to leave Germany for any country that would take them in. My Uncle Berthold, his wife Lisl, and their young son Peter settled in Amsterdam. Others waited anxiously for their quota number to come up for admission to the United States or for a visa from England. Günter tried to emigrate, but to no avail. The relatives and friends we had abroad were not sufficiently settled to be in a position to provide a visa stating that they would guarantee the support of one person, let alone a family.

Many public places were closed to Jews, and the sign, *Juden unerwünscht* (Jews not welcome), became a familiar sight. Vati became more and more depressed, while Mutti tried to be her usual cheerful self. My parents went out less often and entertained their friends at home. Slowly but surely, Germany was preparing for war. The people were all told to economize. One Sunday a month was designated for *Eintopfgericht*, meaning that you had to cook a simple meal in one pot only and donate the savings to the 'Fatherland'. The iron railings bordering the lawns on streets and parks – on which we had perfected our balancing act – disappeared. We were asked to save toothpaste tubes and other aluminium. Signs for air raid shelters appeared overnight, and we even had drills with sirens droning. Everybody had to go into the cellars or designated shelters until the all-clear siren sounded. Where were the Western Powers? Neither the German people nor the Free World suspected that Hitler was preparing for war.

Dorit and I were no longer able to play our games and socialize. She had to wear the uniform of the Nazi-sponsored 'BDM' *Bund Deutscher Mädchen* (Union of German Girls), and I was told to pretend not to know her whenever she was in the company of Aryan girls. I felt crushed, not being able to acknowledge my friend, and I missed her company. Once in a while, she would sneak up the dark and winding *Hintertreppe* (backstairs) of our apartment house to visit me.

I now attended the *Mittelschule der Jüdischen Gemeinde*, which was situated in East Berlin in the Grosse Hamburger Strasse. A few Jewish girls I knew went to Jewish private schools which sprang up like mushrooms when Jewish children were no longer allowed to attend the public schools. My parents were in no position to pay for private schooling for me, so I took the trip on the *Stadtbahn* (S-Bahn – elevated train) every morning except Saturdays. Even on Sunday, I had to get up at 6 am, heat the cocoa my mother left for me on the kitchen table, eat my roll, and walk the deserted streets to the Charlottenburg Station to reach Oranienburgerstrasse, the stop after Friedrichstrasse, past the Reichstag and Unter den

Linden. The schoolbuilding was behind a beautiful synagogue (Oranienburgerstrasse), the largest synagogue in Berlin.
It was built in Eastern style, with a huge, very imposing
cupola. A Jewish cemetery which adjoined the school,
contained the grave of the famous philosopher, Moses
Mendelssohn.

I liked school well enough; it was quite a challenge. Classes
started at 8 am and ran to approximately 3 pm. We had many
subjects, including English, French, and Hebrew. I liked
English best because our teacher, Frau Rosner, would make
the lessons very graphic. A rotund lady with grey curly hair
and glasses, she would raise her arms skywards and declaim,
'and the bridge goes up' (meaning the famous Tower Bridge,
of course), then her arms would come down with the rest of
her upper torso and she concluded: 'and the bridge comes
down'. Thereupon, she straightened up, stomped across the
room with the next line: 'and the friend would walk over the
bridge'. The class giggled discreetly into their handkerchiefs.
In spite of her teaching, I liked the language and persuaded
my parents to let me join a conversation class given privately
in the neighbourhood. I was the youngest in the group, but I
picked up a few phrases which stood me in good stead later
on.

Some people and personalities teaching at the Grosse
Hamburger Strasse, stand out in my mind, and I remember
most of the subjects I learned at the age of ten or eleven.
One of them was ancient history, taught by a tiny, bird-
like woman, humpbacked and shrunken, with a large nose,
penetrating eyes covered by thick glasses and wavy grey
hair pulled tightly into a bun. Her gnarled hands held a walking cane. She was Frau Doktor Reissmann, and she obviously
was an expert in her subject. If I remember any history at all,
it was her version of the Phoenicians, Greeks, and Romans,
their many wars and the rich cultures of their ancient king-
doms.

With the new school came new friends. First there was the group who rode the *Stadtbahn* with me and boarded the train at the same station, and then there were those who joined us at further stops along the way. We formed a little clique that huddled together and threw glances at the group of boys who also rode the same train to school. Boys were taught separately in an adjacent building, and we did not mix. Of course, we were growing up and our interest in the opposite sex was burgeoning, more so in some than in others. We whispered and gossiped about our male fellow pupils and pretended to follow them in order to catch their conversation. Naturally, they ignored us completely.

I had many girl-friends at school: Marianne, Dörte, Eva, Elisabeth, and Ursel. Some of them lived in different neighbourhoods, and I had to travel by *U-Bahn* (underground), bus, or *S-Bahn* to visit them. Sometimes I was allowed to sleep over with my friend, Eva Z., who lived in Neukölln above a little store her parents ran, a hat-cleaning business. I was fascinated by the forms and the steam machines. Apart from learning about the hat-cleaning process, Eva shared with me her knowledge of sex. For the first time, I heard about condoms and learned to recognize them when discarded in the parks. At home sex was never mentioned. It was a topic that did not concern children.

Another girl I visited quite often was Elisabeth S. Her father was a physician and they lived in a large apartment in a very nice neighbourhood. Lisa was a tomboy. She owned an air rifle which she taught me how to use. We drew pictures of our teachers, amongst them Frau Rosner, the English teacher, and used them for target practice. A rather cruel sport, but lots of fun!

From Lisa and her cousin Ilse – who was two years older and went to a different school – I learned all about the American Indians. We pored over the lengthy and detailed books of Karl Mai, a German romantic author who wrote with great authority about the Red Indians of the American Wild West, their way of life, character, and dealings with settlers who were out to conquer their lands. 'Old Shatterhand' was the hero who dealt fairly with the noble chiefs and their tribes. We had deep admiration for these brave men who were decked out in leather and feather headdresses, smoked peace pipes, and spoke in monosyllables: 'Ugh'.

It became our game. Not only did we read all the Karl Mai volumes we could lay our hands on, but also James Fenimore Cooper's *Lederstrumpf* (Leatherstocking Tales) was popular. We purchased clay pipes, which we passed around in a secret location and smoked with great solemnity. Ilse managed to appropriate some tobacco from her pipe-smoking father. We also made our own bows from willow rods and fashioned arrows from branches which we feathered and tipped with glass shards or stones.

Most Saturdays we rode on the *U-Bahn* to Grunewald, the large natural park that adjoins Berlin. The woods are mainly composed of pines and conifers, since the ground is dry and sandy. Their branches start rather high up, however, we managed to find some on which we could test our climbing skills. Didn't Indians always climb the highest trees to observe their enemies and spot the game? We even discovered that some enterprising person had driven stakes into the trunk of a high fir tree at equal distances apart, which enabled us to climb to the top branches. Of course, our parents were not aware of our dangerous adventures. They visited the Grunewald on Sundays in the summer for walking in the fragrant air and for afternoon coffee. At a designated café one could brew one's own coffee and use the tables and chairs. People carried their own pots, mugs and coffee. Of course, the inevitable *Kuchen* (cake) was not forgotten. For what is coffee without cake?

Günter frequented the *Sportsplatz* (Sports Arena) in the Grunewald. He was a sprinter and belonged to a Jewish sportsclub. On occasion, he would take me with him to watch him run track. He provided a seat for me on the crossbar of his bicycle by cushioning it with a pillow. It wasn't too comfortable, but I enjoyed the outings and liked to watch the sports, the running, discus and javelin throwing, as well as the high and long jump. The Jewish schools also held their sports days at this stadium, and once I participated in a relay race.

In February of 1938 my parents celebrated their 25th wedding anniversary. It was a glorious celebration and the plans were made well in advance. We spent the morning visiting 'Sans Souci', Frederick II's palace in Potsdam and then took a taxi to a fine restaurant for lunch. In the afternoon friends and neighbours came in for coffee and cake, while in the evening my parents, brother and I had tickets for the variety show at the Wintergarten, a large concert hall in the West End. How excited I was! My ever thoughtful Tante Käthe bought me a dress for the occasion, a blue wool dress, embroidered Hungarian-style around the front opening, the collar and cuffs and down the sleeves. How elegant I felt in this beautiful dress! It became my favourite for many years to come and luckily it was big enough to fit me for a while.

To surprise my father, a large *Baumkuchen* was delivered to the apartment. Shaped like a tree trunk, this tree cake is baked on a constantly turning dowel. It is made by alternating thin layers of marzipan and cake dough and ultimately covering it with a glaze of chocolate or vanilla. One must slice it horizontally into very skinny portions to savour the flavour. As a rule, we purchased just one thick slice, for it was rather an expensive treat. Since it was my father's favourite confectionery a large cake, at least a foot high, was ordered. Another treat was the taxi that we took to the restaurant. With the exception of my Uncle Max, nobody I knew owned a car, and who took taxis? Certainly not my frugal parents! Also, having a meal in a restaurant was something reserved for special occasions.

The show at the Wintergarten was also a first for me. I was very impressed by the huge auditorium with its vaulted ceiling resembling a sky with tiny bulbs twinkling like millions of stars. One of the performers was the famous clown 'Grogg'. He was known for his declamation, *'Eine Brücke, eine Brücke!'* (A bridge, a bridge) I still don't know what he meant by that, but it comes to mind with his name. The other acts were of the circus variety: juggling, acrobatics, animal acts, etc. It was the most exciting day I had ever experienced!

After the joyful anniversary celebration and following the departure of my beloved Aunt Käthe and Uncle Richard, I celebrated my 12th birthday. Mutti made me the customary party. My girl-friends came dressed in taffeta party dresses bearing gifts. We lit one thick birthday candle and everyone sang the appropriate song: *Hoch sollst du leben* (Long may you live).

It was 1938, the year before the war. The position of the Jews became more and more precarious since the Nuremberg Laws had been passed and gradually amended and enforced. In the parks, a few benches were painted yellow and those were assigned to Jews. *Juden Verboten* signs sprang up everywhere. The lucky ones departed to other countries, but I don't believe that my parents made serious efforts to leave, knowing that Vati was considered a cripple. Besides, he tenaciously held to the belief that having given his arm for the Fatherland, he was immune from persecution.

The few relatives who had managed to emigrate were not in a position to send visas for us. Günter, as he later told me, was desperate to leave Germany. He finally received a student visa through the efforts of mother's cousin Walter, who had established himself in London with his family. As Günter told the story, he waited anxiously at the German Emigration Office to have his visa validated. The official hesitated to affix the necessary certification, and Günter's heart sank. As luck would have it, the man was called away from his desk at that moment, and when he returned, he absent-mindedly affixed the crucial stamp of approval on the document. Günter practically bolted out of the office. Soon afterwards he departed to London.

In June of that year, the Nazis arbitrarily arrested a large group of male Jews whom they transported to Sachsenhausen, not far from Berlin, one of the first concentration camps. My Uncle Max was amongst them. The men, their hair shorn, were put into prison suits, and subjected to hard labour, abuse, and bad food. Most of them were released a month or two later, but the harsh treatment had taken its toll. Max, who came to visit after his release was a broken man. Merely in his fifties, he looked more like 80, with grey stubbles on his head and his back bent. He was put to nap on the daybed in the study while his wife, Edith, visited.

Our family doctor, Erich W. was also among those arrested. His practice had been restricted to Jewish patients since Hitler's laws. But in July, no Jewish doctors were allowed to practise any more. In panic, his wife, Else, asked us to accommodate her and their child while they waited for their American quota number to come up. Their 'lift' (huge trunk) was packed and they were ready to leave at a moment's notice. Else and her daughter, Marianne, moved into my parents' large bedroom while they relocated their own beds to the formerly elegant Green Salon. I was delighted to have a 'little sister' and although Marianne was two years younger than me, we enjoyed each other's company. We had fun playing hide-and-seek around the house and climbing on top of the trunks and suitcases. They did not stay long. As soon as Erich was released from concentration camp, they obtained a visa from their family in England, wisely anticipating that their American quota number might come up too late for them to depart.

The summer of 1938 was upon us, and it had been arranged that I spend a few weeks in Amsterdam with Mother's brother Berthold, his wife Lisl, and little boy Peter, who had been living there since 1936. I was put on the train in Berlin with my suitcase and sandwiches for the nine-hour train journey. At the border, I had to go through the usual customs inspection; otherwise the trip was fun for me. My uncle and aunt met me in Amsterdam. They lived in an apartment which bordered a huge park-like square with the jawbreaking name of '*Van Tuyll van Seeros Kerkeplein*'. How proud I was to be able to memorize the address! Aunt Lisl was born without a hand, but I marvelled at how competently she was handling all the chores as well as knitting sweaters for Peter with one needle tucked under her arm. My Uncle Berthold was an engineer. He worked in an office in the Heerengracht, bordering one of those canals not far from the house where Anne Frank was to hide in later years. Peter was six years old and attended a Montessori school. They had adapted to their new homeland, spoke Dutch pretty well, and had Dutch friends. I loved going shopping with my aunt, since the good-natured shopkeepers always offered a treat to the children, a piece of candy at the grocery, a slice of sausage at the butcher's, a cookie at the bakery. I learned to ask for ice cream on luscious round waffle sandwiches topped with optional whipped cream. We spent many sunny days in the sand-dunes nearby, but I also saw the seashore and colourful villages where people wore their native costumes and wooden clogs.

On rainy days I ventured on the tram into the centre of Amsterdam to hunt for Shirley Temple pictures, paper dolls, and whatever I could purchase with my limited funds of Dutch guilder. After a three-week stay, I was put on the train back to Berlin loaded down with Dutch chocolate, ginger-bread (which was my father's favourite), coffee, and cocoa. At the border, the official was most cooperative and suggested that I brew some coffee before I got home since I had brought a few ounces more than the allowed export limit.

School started again and I went back to my routine and lots of homework. There were many letters from Günter. He had settled down in England and had a job with a textile firm. He was trying to contact people who could be helpful in getting us out of Germany, but he had little luck. However, he managed to make a contact for his childhood friend, Hans, who joined him in London and who in turn successfully saved his sister Marion from the impending Holocaust.

In August 1938 the Nazis had decreed that all Jews had to add the name 'Sara' or 'Israel' to their given names, and they were issued a *Kennkarte* (identity card) with their photo, new name, and stamped with a big 'J'. My parents tried to shield me from their worries.

One day in October I went to school as usual, only to find that one-third of the girls in my class were absent. We were told that those families of Polish origin had been sent back to Poland. It was hard for me to comprehend; no prior notice, no preparation, no goodbyes, just uprooted and deported. No one knew at the time that they had been taken to Zbaszyn, a desolate bordertown in Poland or of the misery that awaited them.

This was the dawning of *Kristallnacht*, November 9. Our friendly boarder, Müllerchen, had by that time already moved his electronic equipment to safety. He knew that he could no longer stay in a Jewish home. The night of terror began with loud banging and the sound of broken glass. Downstairs, the Nazis smashed the printing machines of the corner store. My parents locked and bolted our heavy front door. Across the street was a stationery store run by two sisters. Scared to death, they sought refuge in our apartment in their night clothes. My parents admitted them after recognizing them through the peephole. We huddled together, terrified. I clung to my mother, who tried her best to remain calm. At any moment we expected the SS men to break down the door. Towards morning, things quietened down and I was persuaded to go back to bed. Someone informed us that all the synagogues were burning. Little did we know that this was happening all over Germany by prior arrangement.

A few days later, I went back to school, making my way around the glass, broken machinery, and scattered window displays littering the sidewalks. While riding the *S-Bahn*, I saw the smouldering ruins of the synagogue on Fasanen-strasse, which is located quite close to the overhead railroad tracks. What a terrifying sight! Not many children showed up at school, and we were sent home.

My father gave Günter an account of what had happened in the following letter:

> Dear Boy,
>
> I am hardly able to think a clear thought since what came upon us Jews in Germany at four-thirty this morning is simply indescribable. No synagogue exists any-more in the whole of Germany which was not burned down or is burning. No display windows exist which were not destroyed. At N.J.'s (store), all windows were broken by 2 P.M. at Arnold Müller, they broke twelve, at Hermanns and Froitzheimer's, seven, etc. etc.
>
> What happened to the window displays you can imagine. And what will follow this? But what can one do; one sits bound in a cage and must endure it all.

I added a few lines to my father's outpouring, telling Günter that I was well (except for the dots that I used to express my shock at what had happened). I added that I had not gone to school for a few days, saying that Mutti was afraid.

Mutti's letter was written soon afterwards:

> I will never forget this St. Bartholomew night [a six-teenth-century religious blood-bath in France] as long as I live. The banging, thunderlike crashing and shouting,

was unbelievable. It destroyed something deep inside of me. It destroyed my belief in Humanity. We live amongst savages, my boy. One saw people unmasked, base, and mean, enjoying the destruction. I can't get rid of the feeling that this was done on order. We, Mrs Wolffenstein and I, are not allowing the children to go to school until Monday because 'The Churning *Volksseele'* [Folksoul] could flare up again. And this is just the beginning. Therefore I beg you at least to save your sister before it is too late.

If the conscience of the world does not wake up soon, we are lost. We are not even safe in our homes. The child was so shook up today that she cried bitterly. It hurt my innermost soul, believe me. And for all this, your father carries his wooden arm, and the hand he lost wore the iron ring with the inscription: 'The Fatherland's Thanks'.

Günter's reply came promptly in the form of a telegram to my parents: 'Send Annemarie out immediately'. He had found an English Jewish family that was willing to take me in for the sum of one pound weekly, which a friend of his, Franz – more affluent than Günter – generously offered to pay for my keep. Organizations and private groups in England started to work feverishly to save as many children as possible.

My parents registered me for the *Kindertransporte* which were arranged with great speed. Mother prepared the clothing I was to take with me. Everything was bought or made with future growth in mind, as the clothes had to last a while. The hems were huge and the sleeves had tucks. Mutti also prepared me for my impending womanhood by packing sanitary napkins and explaining their use when the need would arise. I was only allowed one suitcase, but a trunk was packed with linens, some books, and of course my beloved 'Kätie-doll'. This was sent to England later. December 28 was my departure date. There were hugs, kisses, and tears, but I was

11 Vati and Mutti on the Balcony

sure that eventually Vati and Mutti would follow us to England and we would all be reunited. They saw me off on the train to Hamburg where we were to take the boat to Southampton.

I did not know it, but I was an orphan from that day on.

2 • England

The tears had been shed at the railway station where the children were assembled, tagged, and labelled, dragging their rucksacks, suitcases, dolls, stuffed animals and musical instruments. Fathers and mothers hid their grief as best they could. There were hugs and kisses, white handkerchiefs fluttering from open windows of train compartments. It was December 28, and a group of children were on their way to Hamburg and then on to England. The people in charge of this *Kindertransport* of approximately 100 had the responsibility of herding the group from the train onto the ocean liner anchored in Hamburg's harbour.

This was one of the earlier transports leaving for England. Little did we know that the British were to rescue 10,000 children between December 1938 and September 1939. The Home Office had approved this undertaking and many brave individuals volunteered to organize the evacuation. Only children unaccompanied by their parents to the age of 17 were to be admitted. Foster homes were found – both Jewish and Gentile – hostels were opened, boarding schools contacted and established summer camp facilities were readied to receive these children. It was a tremendous undertaking, and all of us owe our lives to this venture. If only America had followed suit, many more Jewish children could have been saved.

It was cold and damp on the deck of the *SS Washington*, passenger ship of the Hamburg–America Line. Chunks of ice were floating in the harbour. In order to cheer up a group of little girls, I pulled my Hohner harmonica from my pocket and proceeded to play some popular folk songs. *Nun adee du mein lieb' Heimatland* (Now Goodbye to You My Dear Homeland) came to mind. We didn't realize that the goodbyes were final. We would not see our homeland so soon again.

Below deck, the cabin – to which four girls had been assigned – was stuffy and confining. It held two bunk beds and a washbasin. I knew one of the girls. She had been a schoolmate of mine at the Jewish School in Berlin. The others were strangers, but not for long. We were literally 'all in the same boat' together. I climbed on the top bunk and tried to loosen the tightly tucked blankets and sheets. It was to no avail. Once in bed, I pushed my big toe right through the sheet.

We discovered that each one of us had a different language skill, so that if a stranger should knock on our cabin door, we would be able to address this person in English, French, German or Hebrew. I was assigned to speak in English, having studied it in school, as well as privately. My three bunkmates had scant knowledge of the two other languages. But no foreign stranger ever knocked on our door.

It was a rough crossing. Whoever said that you can't get seasick if you stand on deck and look down into the swirling water, was wrong, dead wrong. We were all seasick. No matter what I tried, standing on the freezing deck, lying on my bunk bed, eating, not eating, I felt miserable. On arriving in Southampton the next day, I still felt nauseous on the train to London.

The children were processed on arrival at the railway station in London, underwent a cursory medical examination and were then released to relatives and friends, or assigned to a camp at Dovercourt, on the East coast.

I was one of the lucky ones. My brother Günter met me. It is a wonder that he recognized me in my oversized brown tweed coat with the dyed Persian lamb collar of which I was so proud. I was carrying a dreadful brown cardboard suitcase.

12 Arrival in London, December 1938

All the clothes that my mother had packed were on the large side, made to grow into. Amongst them was a navy wool dress trimmed with red and white braid, and my favourite, the soft blue embroidered dress which Aunt Käthe had bought for me. Much later I cut it down and wore it as a blouse. It survived many washings and the attacks from moths. I could never part with it, and for years it lay in that same cardboard suitcase in the attic.

My other belongings, shipped in a large trunk, arrived later. Mutti had packed sheets, a pillow, huge cases for non-existent featherbeds, her own linen tablecloths bordered with hand crocheted lace, a few books and games, and of course my beloved Kätie-doll.

It was a happy reunion with Günter. He felt the responsibility of having to care for me very keenly, and although he was inexperienced in raising a budding teenager, he told me in all seriousness that he was going to be both father and mother to me. My mother's cousin, Walter Jackman, had emigrated in 1937 and lived in London. Günter thought it best to take me there temporarily. Walter had lost his first wife and had recently married Vera, in order to give his two children, Erika and Gerald, a mother.

Erika and I had formed a friendship in Germany, prior to their leaving for England. Our closest tie was our love for Shirley Temple. We were avid collectors of pictures, clippings and anything at all to do with the movie star. We exchanged postcards and pictures, just as Dorit and I had done at home. After Erika's departure for London, I sent her paper dolls and any newspaper and magazine clippings I could spare, for her scrapbook. Erika also saw every Shirley Temple film several times and learned all the songs which she sang in English as well as in the German translation.

Walter and Vera lived in Wembley, a residential part of London, in a small bright detached house with a small front lawn surrounded by hedges. A few steps led up to the front entrance. English people savour their privacy. They don't have front porches or sit on their front steps. All activities take place in the back garden where shrubs or fences enclose the property.

Erika greeted me with a Kit Kat bar, which promptly became my favourite chocolate snack. She had become very British, since she went to a public school and wore the prescribed schoolgirl uniform: white blouse with tie, pleated gym-slip with woven belt and a floppy black velour hat trimmed with a ribbon of the school colours. It suited her well with her short dark hair, sparkling brown eyes and dimples.

The first evening of my arrival, I was left at the house by myself, as the family had reservations for the circus. There was no ticket for me. Why had it not occurred to them to buy another ticket? As a consolation, Vera left me with a plate of assorted cookies and candy. I ate the cookies, but was not consoled and cried with homesickness as I stuffed them into my mouth.

It was not a happy household. Erika and Gerald resented their stepmother, Vera. She was strong-minded and strict and ruled with an iron hand. For breakfast, she would carefully arrange sliced bread on a plate, an equal number of buttered slices and those spread with jam. There was one of each for us. I had never experienced this before. At home, we could have whatever we wanted, butter or jam. Vera also counted out the cookies for us with great care: one chocolate, one plain, one wrapped, one iced. I was used to making my own choices and felt very strange with this arrangement.

My cousins soon found a way to avenge themselves. They raided the pantry, helped themselves to cookies, raisins and nuts, and dipped their fingers into jams and preserves. I quickly learned to join them.

After a week or so, I was shipped off to Neasden to the British family with whom I was to stay. Mr and Mrs Pincus received the magnificent sum of one pound per week for my room and board. This was provided by my brother's affluent friend, Franz. I was given a small room in their modest home containing a bed, dresser and wardrobe. This was to be 'home' for the time being.

The Pincus family included the rotund Mrs Pincus, thin, bespectacled Mr Pincus, their son Johnny – who was about a year younger than me – and, to my delight, a little sleek black dog named *Kleiner* (little one). This little mutt was a car-chaser who made my blood run cold several times with his close encounters with moving vehicles.

Johnny was short for his age, neither fat nor skinny, with dirty-blond hair and a nasal voice. He sounded as though he had a perpetual cold. I suppose he resented me, since he was an only child and not used to competition in the home. He took his anger out on me by being mean and teasing me. Johnny was the picture of a typical English schoolboy, dressed in grey shorts, a grey pullover, grey blazer, grey cap, grey knee socks, black shoes, and a striped school tie. He attended a public (private) school, while I was sent to the (public) County Council school.

I tried to keep out of Johnny's way. One day, when his parents were out, he managed to lock us both in the bathroom. In our scuffle the key slipped under the door. We thought of tearing up sheets from the linen closet to make an escape ladder, but thought better of it and waited to be released.

The winter of 1938–39 was cold and damp, and I could not pile enough wool blankets onto my bed to keep warm in my unheated room. I longed for my featherbed. Finally, Erika's family lent me one which I lugged home happily on the bus stuffed into a big sack.

Mrs Pincus was kind enough to me, but she was no replacement for my mother, nor could her house replace our comfortable apartment with its elegant Green Salon, central heating and other comforts. She liked to lounge in bed in the morning and would call out to me before I went to school:

'Marie, bring me up a cup of tea.'

She used only half of my given name, as though it was too much effort to pronounce my whole name, Annemarie.

That January of 1939, I was enrolled at the Borough of Willesden School, Wykeham School, which took children from the age of five until they left at 14 to learn a trade or find employment. My English language skills improved gradually, and I was able to make myself understood. However, my vocabulary was still sketchy, and when we read *The Wind in the Willows* in class, it was only a few years later that I realized what a 'badger' was, let alone the other animals.

My teacher, a tiny dark-haired Welsh woman, Miss Rathbone, was very kind and helpful to me. At the end of the second term she rewarded me with a gift of the book *Little Women*. The classes at Wykeham School were quite large, and the teachers maintained strict discipline. If the children were restless, Miss Rathbone would call out:

'Hands behind your backs! Hands on the table! Hands on your heads!'

It was like a game of 'Simon Says'. We also had to memorize the multiplication tables, as the numbers were fired at us very rapidly: 6×4, 3×5, 9×7, etc., like shots from a rifle.

Apart from the academic subjects, we all participated in Physical Education classes where we played 'rounders', and also had Music lessons, in which we sang folksongs accompanied on the piano by the teacher. Miss Rathbone, like so many Welsh natives, had a beautiful voice. As much as I enjoyed her singing in the music class, Home Economics was my favourite class. It took place in a large, airy room, lined with green ceramic tiles and surrounded by push-aside windows. There were several stoves and sinks around the sides of the classroom while in the middle there were a dozen neatly arranged wooden tables and chairs. Here I learned not only how to plan a day of housework, but also how to bake 'rock cakes', roll pastry dough, scrub tables and not least, the correct way to iron a shirt.

I remained a mystery to my classmates. Since I didn't speak the language fluently and often had to translate what they said into German, they would raise their voices, thinking I was merely deaf. I would respond:

'Don't cry. I understand.' (In German, *schreien* means to cry as well as to shout.)

There was another refugee from Germany in my class, a girl named Mia. We gravitated to each other like iron filings to a magnet, happy to be together and able to speak our own language, to gossip or to laugh secretly at the behaviour of the British, which we found so strange. We also discussed our foster families. In the summer that followed, Mia and I spent many hours at the local swimming pool. The temperature was cool by American standards and the water was quite chilly, but when in England, one soon learns to take advantage of every ray of sunshine. It is like a rare gift.

Sunday was always special. I looked forward to it all week. On that day I would visit Günter at his 'digs' (lodgings), where he shared a large room with his childhood friend, Hans, and another young man, Johnny, with whom I promptly fell in love. He was tall and handsome, very dark complexioned, with black hair and a jaunty black moustache, which I watched him touch up with black paste that looked like shoe polish. I don't know what attracted me more, Johnny or the moist fruitcake with big red cherries that the landlady served for breakfast.

Günter, now 21 years old, was working for a textile firm in the days before the war, doing odd jobs and learning the business. He prided himself on taking good care of me. He supplied me with pocket money and never failed to ask me if I needed anything. I doubt that he was aware of how desperately I missed my mother. Anyway, he tried his best. On many Sundays, he would take me with him wherever he was going. We would often visit friends or one of his many girl-friends. I didn't like the ones who fussed over me. Occasionally, I had to wait outside while he picked up a girl at her place or saw her to the door.

He also introduced me to the Loewenthals, a refugee family with two daughters. The older one, Ursula or Ulla – as we called her – and I were the same age and soon became fast friends. This family, with the exception of Ulla, was extremely obese. Mr Loewenthal was heavy-set, with a large lion-like head. He travelled a great deal and therefore was not at home very often. Ulla and I frequented his extensive library and found books that were not considered suitable for thirteen-year-olds. Mrs L was very romantic. She never tired of telling us about her youth in Germany, her admirers, flirtations, the dances she attended, and the frilly clothes she wore. It didn't mean very much to Ulla or me. We didn't care for these things. The younger daughter, Anne, was so chubby and ungainly that, in our estimation, she was hardly a candidate for fun and games with the opposite sex, which also held little interest for us.

Although I was always aware of being an outsider, I found a certain measure of warmth and mothering in this family. Ulla and I tumbled on the grass in her small back yard, stood on our heads, and climbed onto the garage, where we sat like stone gargoyles. We enjoyed being tomboys.

At this time in the spring and summer of 1939, there were weekly letters from home crossing the channel, also packages with all kinds of necessities. Günter apparently had asked for razor blades, soap, toothpaste and talcum powder. Mutti also sent him his spring coat and pyjamas. She wanted to know if she should have his black shoes repaired. Obviously, she realized that he was very low on funds. My parents' letters expressed their despair and longing to be reunited with their children. Both Vati and Mutti implored Günter to make some contacts which would help them obtain a permit to emigrate to England. They must have mentioned to their friends, too, their disappointment that Günter had not been successful in advancing their cause, because in June, he received a devastating letter from Müllerchen, whom they had met in the street. He took it upon himself to present my parents' situation rather harshly. He accused Günter of not making his parents his priority and warned him that it may soon be too late and he would regret it forever. Although Müller could not foresee the pending Holocaust and the annihilation of 6,000,000 Jews, he painted a graphic picture of two desperate people ending up on the street while he, Günter, pursued his pleasures and passions and even expected packages and gifts. He claimed that were he in his shoes, he would work day and night to find a way to obtain a permit.

'Your conscience will bother you all your life', he wrote, 'soon your parents' letters will have a different ring.'

This postscript was directed to me: 'It would be quite proper to let your sister read this letter, so she should be informed as well.'

Müller was right. This letter must have weighed heavily on Günter's conscience all his life. He never showed it to me or talked about it. I did not find it until after his death in 1984. Yes, the tone of my parents' letters changed drastically. Vati wrote to Günter the day after Müller had dashed off his impassioned letter. He also could not suppress his feelings of disappointment and dissatisfaction at the delay of their departure, his resentment at being told to keep his chin up and the seemingly empty promise that Günter would contact yet another potential guarantor.

> I asked you to get in touch with Governor Lehmann in New York, [he wrote] What did you do? Nothing. You promised to arrange everything, but you don't even sacrifice your lunch hour or your free evenings.

Father quoted names of sons and daughters who had managed to get their parents out of Germany and begged Günter not to dismiss his pleas but to give it at least one hour of serious consideration.

Within a week, a devastated Günter wrote, full of apologies and regrets, and by that time, Vati had rued his outburst and answered:

> We understand your difficulties only too well. We don't want to portray you as a criminal, but it would help if you shared your problems and disappointments with us so we don't have false hopes. Our life is already hard enough so that we can bear any unpleasantness as long as it is not kept secret from us.

Mutti filled up the other side of the paper with her beautiful handwriting.

> My dear boy, [she wrote] Wouldn't it be terrible if we failed to understand you, after all we have known you for such a long time! [Affectionately, she continued] You are our Huschi-Puschi (scatterbrain) who is unfortunately on the gullible side and already has the sparrows in his hands when they are still sitting on the roof. Do you have problems at work? Is your employment endangered? We realize you have difficulties, and due to the distance we don't communicate our problems either. But in order to understand each other better, we should share our concerns.

She also wrote that she had invited Müller for coffee and he had told her about the letter he had written. She resented his writing to Günter. They had been in such despair at that particular time, but Müller had no right to interfere.

The letters kept coming, more and more suggestions on how to obtain this all-important permit, how to find a guarantor, even two or three. Vati also referred to a telephone call from us in London, which pleased them but did not satisfy them altogether. He expressed pessimism about the political situation. Who could rely on France to cross the whole continent to come to Poland's aid? And he could not really believe in Günter's statement that England had never yet lost a war. With great foresight, he also voiced the thought that Russia was playing a double game and could not be trusted.

That summer, Günter took me with him to Westgate-on-Sea on the East coast for a week's vacation. It made me feel very grown-up to be taken along by this handsome young man, my brother, who was very much the dandy with his flannel slacks, open shirt, and silk kerchief. We stayed in a private house, where he had rented rooms. The days were spent on the beach, Günter sitting in a deck-chair reading, while I splashed in the water or dug holes in the sand. We borrowed bikes and rode around the little town or walked on the top of the magnificent white cliffs that are so famous, particularly in Dover, and stretch southward along the coastline. Longingly, I gazed across the channel which divided us from the Continent, from Berlin, from home. I wanted to share this lovely seashore with my parents, but all I could do, was to try to express my thoughts in letters or send picture postcards.

Vati wrote that he was happy for us to be free and to live amongst free people. The situation was becoming extremely difficult for them, since he was now without a job. He was forced to spend many hours at the unemployment office in long lines, writing resumés and collecting references. They relied on the income from the rooms they rented out, and even that became more and more difficult, since many Jews found themselves in a position similar to that of my parents. The hope of getting out of Germany was slowly fading, and neither Vati nor Mutti could buy their son's optimism any longer. Vati warned Günter not to enter into any agreement that could threaten his own future without consulting older and more knowledgeable people.

The letters addressed to me were written in a different vein. The longing to hug and kiss me, to cuddle and spoil me was part of every other sentence. Of course, I was reminded to be good and brave and to love my brother.

Something else crept into their letters as time went on, an abandonment to fate, an apprehension of what was to come, and a trust in God, a last hope that He, who had been driven away from their community (literal translation), would care for all the poor uprooted people. Mutti wrote: 'I commit you to the protection of the heavens, to the God who makes no deals and compromises.'

By the time autumn came, Hitler had annexed the Sudetenland and Czechoslovakia in the same manner as Austria. There were rumours of an impending German invasion, of paratroopers dropping from the sky. The British people had to practise a complete blackout routine. One evening, I had taken a bus home from Ulla's house and had to rely on the conductor to let me off at the right stop. It was pitch dark, every window being covered with dark curtains. Not even the street lights were turned on. London felt strange, and it was hard to find one's way.

In school we were told to prepare for evacuation. Everyone was issued a gas mask in a square cardboard box strung with cord to hang over our shoulders. We had endured several drills, breathing in acrid fumes of rubber and noting that we looked like pigs with black snouts. The children were required to bring a knapsack with clothing to school every day, so as to be ready for evacuation from London at a moment's notice.

Finally, the fateful day came. We were loaded onto buses. It was September 3, 1939. Hitler had marched into Poland. War had been declared.

3 • Evacuee

The buses deposited us at the railway station, where we boarded a train. Where we were going, nobody could tell us. As we passed small stations, we strained to see the names of the towns, but in vain, for all signs had been blackened out. The British were concerned about an enemy invasion by parachute and had thought to thoroughly confuse the invaders by not revealing any locations.

After about an hour's ride, we were hustled off the train and lined up. We found ourselves in a medium-sized town which we discovered to be Bedford. There we were issued with a shopping bag containing goodies, including a supersized thick bar of Cadbury's milk chocolate, my favourite! There was also a square can of bully beef (corned beef from Argentina), and other groceries not to be eaten immediately.

Loaded down with a suitcase or knapsack, gas mask, and shopping bag, we were divided into groups of 20 or 30 children, assigned to two teachers, and sent off into the unknown. As luck would have it, the group in which I found myself was accompanied by Miss Rathbone, the Welsh teacher from Wykeham School and a tall handsome blonde, Miss Smith.

Our bus travelled approximately 20 miles through the English countryside, passing lush green farmland dotted with houses, barns and grazing sheep and cows. We tried to read the signposts, but all the place names had been blocked out. Eventually the bus stopped in front of a stone church and we disembarked. The Vicar and a few of the local ladies welcomed us, and we were soon assigned to various homes in groups of twos and threes. We found out that we were in Swineshead, a village of 100 inhabitants (actually 98, since two young men had enlisted), approximately 20 miles north of Bedford in the county of Bedfordshire and ten miles from the border of Northamptonshire.

Most of the residents owned small farms, and the rest worked for them. The church was in the centre of the village. A combination post-office and convenience store was opposite. There was a pub next door. What more could one ask for? Swineshead had no electricity or plumbing. Drinking water came from pumps, whereas water for washing and cleaning was collected in rain barrels.

My first billet was with the Phillips', the most affluent family in Swineshead, who owned practically all of the village, including a large stone farmhouse with a cobbled yard where the hunt met regularly. The villagers considered Mrs Phillips 'La-di-da', several cuts above them in class, education, speech and dress. Everyone in the village worked for the Phillips' in one way or another. Both teachers lived at their house, as well as another girl from London named Joan, with whom I shared a room. I remember feeling very intimidated by the teachers' presence. My stay there was short. After a few weeks I was moved to a small cottage of a young widow and her baby. Another evacuee, named Pat, was staying there alone, since her roommate had gone home. Pat was a year older than me and very aggressive. She bullied me constantly. She selfishly took up most of the space in the double bed we shared, and I was squeezed to the wall. Luckily this situation did not last long, and I was moved once again, this time to 'Kosycott', a thatched cottage a short way out of the village. My hosts were the Manfields, Mary and Jim. There were two other girls in the house already, Joyce and Daphne, but I got along with them and with 'Aunt' Mary and 'Uncle' Jim, as we called them.

The Manfields had two sons, Harold and John. Harold had

13 The Manfields

joined the Marines, and John stayed home to help run the small farm. Aunt Mary was a kind 'no-nonsense' woman in her fifties. She had been a nurse in the First World War, and there were many pictures around the house to prove it. She dealt with us firmly but with loving kindness, and I grew very fond of her. But Uncle Jim was the one who stole my heart completely. He was a sinewy man, stooped, with gnarled hands and weather-beaten skin. He had a pleasant disposition and an engaging though toothless smile. His wife affectionately called him 'My Ducky', and I called him that too.

John was a husky, good-looking lad of about 20, who took great pleasure in teasing us girls, occasionally tossing dead animals into our room, and generally making sure that something sent us screaming into the countryside, whereupon he would burst into raucous laughter. John's constant companion was Joey, a black and brown mutt that must have had retriever blood, since he was always ready to go hunting with

14 The Village School

John. Harold was a few years older than John and more gentle. I liked him a lot and felt sorry that he had to be the one to leave for the service and not John.

Every day, we attended classes at the church hall, which served as the one-room schoolhouse. The two teachers, Miss Rathbone and Miss Smith, divided the children – the evacuees as well as the 20 village children – into learning groups and circulated between them. Our numbers shrank gradually, as, one by one, the London parents – seeing that there was no invasion or bombing – missed their children and came to take them home. Daphne and Joyce both left the Manfields' for London, and I was the only one left in the house, getting the big bed and the bedroom all to myself.

I loved the simple life on the farm in spite of all its inconveniences. The paraffin lamps – our only source of light – gave off more smell than illumination and had to be filled regularly and the wicks trimmed. Fresh water needed to be pumped from the old iron pump directly outside the front door and lugged inside in large buckets which had a tendency to spill when you were in a hurry. Wood had to be supplied for the fireplace year round, since the fire was kept burning for cooking, baking and heating kettles of water. An iron oven was built in right beside the grate, and it was no mean feat to keep the temperature constant for baking. In the winter we depended on the heat from the fire, the only source of warmth in the house. The toilet facility was an outhouse in the back yard, an inhospitable wooden hut with a built-in bin which held a bucket covered with a round lid. Mrs Manfield supplied toilet tissue by cutting the newspaper and the many farm advertising circulars they received into neat squares and spearing them onto a large hook on the wall. In the winter, it was an effort to leave the warmth of the fire to heed the call of nature, while in the summer the outhouse was invariably a hangout for spiders, flies, and daddy-long-legs.

Upstairs, the bedrooms were equipped with washbasins, jugs, chamberpots, and slop pails which had to be emptied every day. The water in the jug was scooped from the rain barrel. Once a week I dragged a heavy metal tub into my room and several kettles of hot water for a bath. The trick was to stand in this pool of water, as hot as you could bear it, and wash down as far as possible and then up as far as possible before the water cooled. Quite a feat! 'Possible' never got washed.

Churning butter was a regular weekly chore. Mr and Mrs Manfield and I took turns cranking the handle of the barrel-like butterchurn all day, until the little window would be clear, indicating that the cream had separated from the whey. It was now ready to be kneaded with wooden paddles and shaped into patties, weighed, wrapped in waxed paper, and stored for sale. I worked alongside Aunt Mary, learning from her this ancient craft.

There was always work on the farm. Animals as well as the garden and fields had to be tended, wood needed to be chopped, and vegetables gathered. Even on a small farm, the chores never ended. One of the cows gave birth to a bull calf which I called Nicholas, as he was born on St. Nicholas Day, December 6. That was the day the children in Germany would put their shoes outside their bedroom door in the evening and find them filled with goodies in the morning. My mother went along with that very un-Jewish custom and supplied me with candy and cookies on that night.

I later regretted not having learned to milk the cows, but at the time I felt it wiser to plead ignorance, so I was not in danger of being called upon very early in the morning or pulled away from the warm hearth in the evening.

I wrote letters to Günter regularly and gave him detailed accounts of my activities. I enclosed letters to Erika for delivery and I also asked for wool so I could continue my knitting, a favourite pastime on long winter evenings sitting by the hearth. My parents wrote me long accounts filled with details of their lonely life at home. There were few complaints but much advice to both of us. They were particularly concerned about my education. Vati had been able to find employment and two rooms were rented out, so their situation was not as desperate as it had been. Their lives consisted of eating, sleeping, and working, with a walk after supper to aid digestion. Until September 9, the mail reached us directly, after that the letters came via Holland, Sweden, and later, America through the Jablonskis, our former neighbours.

Tante Käthe added her own letters to those she forwarded and once or twice enclosed a dollar for me, which I promptly sent to Günter with this note: 'I am enclosing the dollar which I received from Aunt Käthe on Monday. Please send me sixpence to spend and put the rest in the bank. Of course, you can use it any time if you want to go to the movies or need a smoke.'

I also gave Günter an account of my Chanukah celebration.

61

15 The Favourite Blue Dress

I have not forgotten Chanukah. Mrs Manfield gave me nine coloured candles which I fastened to a board. Then I surrounded them with photos of you, our parents, Aunt Käthe, and Uncle Richard. I will light a new candle each night, say the *brochot* (blessings) and play: *Maos Zur* [Rock of Ages] on my recorder.

Vati and Mutti also remembered Chanukah in their letters. They visualized our celebration at home the previous year, Marianne and I lighting candles, the songs we sang, and how I played some songs on my recorder which I had learned to play at school, and some on my harmonica. Vati wrote:

A glimmer of your candles reached us so far away and in their glow we caught a glimpse of your dear face, which we have so sorely missed for a whole year.

Mutti wrote:

I can hardly address you as my dear little girl, since you have grown and become so sensible. For me, you will always be the little one, the *Nesthäkchen* [fledgling]. In my mind, I experienced the lighting of the candles with you. Let us hope that we can light them together next year. It seems more than a year ago that we were together. It seems like an eternity.

She also worried that my clothing would not fit me anymore and wondered who would supply me with new clothes. All her thoughts were with us, and she tried to live all my adventures and experiences so she could be part of our lives again.

Günter as well as Hans had volunteered for the British Army as soon as war was declared. At first, the army did not know what to do with this odd assortment of intellectuals and professionals who spoke with heavy foreign accents but were willing and anxious to fight for the country that had given them a haven. Eventually they assigned them to ARP (Air Raid Precaution) duties, headquartered at the local library. Their task was delivering messages to other units in London, crisscrossing the blacked-out city. By February 1940, it was decided to accept foreigners in the British forces. The men were sent to a training camp in Richborough, near Sandwich, Kent. This unit became known as the Pioneer Corps.

The war seemed distant to us in Swineshead. On clear nights we could see a faint red glow in the sky in the direction of London. The fires were burning after a night of bombing. One day a stray bomb was discovered in a nearby field. Luckily it had failed to explode and was safely detonated.

Most of the men in the village were air-raid wardens. They would don their steel helmets whenever the faint wail of sirens was heard in the distance, or when Mrs Nicholson, the postmistress, received a telephone message warning of enemy aircraft heading in our direction. She immediately sent one of her numerous children to deliver a note to the wardens on duty. Once, two incendiary bombs landed down someone's chimney. As luck would have it, they also failed to explode and were viewed by all of us with great curiosity.

A company of soldiers had set up a camp on a hill about a mile away and installed an anti-aircraft gun, or 'Ack-Ack' as we called it. Several came into the village to purchase cigarettes or candy at the Post Office store, or they frequented the local pub. Some stopped at the farm for eggs and milk. Mrs Manfield invited two of the young men for dinner at Christmas-time. One of them, by the name of Gordon Swannell, played the flute. He showed me how to hold it and position my mouth over the hole. It was very different from the recorder. It didn't take me long to pick out melodies and my fingers felt at home on the instrument.

Christmas-time was very special in the country. No matter that it was cold and damp and difficult to leave the fireplace, especially when it was time to retreat to the unheated bedroom where the water froze regularly in the pitcher and the rubber hot water bottles were only capable of warming a small area of the damp bed. Preparations for the holidays had already been in hand for a few weeks. Not only had I knitted woollen helmets for the boys in the armed forces, a khaki one for my brother and a navy one for Harold Manfield, but I had also made a vest for 'My Ducky' and crocheted a hot water bottle cover for Aunt Mary. I had learned the skill of knitting and crocheting at school in Berlin.

We decorated the Manfields' house with branches of evergreens, and there was a small Christmas tree in the corner. It had to be quite small because the ceilings were very low. John was forced to duck his head to avoid the wooden beams, which I tried to touch by doing high kicks. Of course, there was a spray of mistletoe hanging from one of the beams near the door. I looked forward to Harold's holiday leave. He looked so handsome in his navy blue uniform with the shiny gold buttons and the red stripes down the side of his trousers. Cunningly I waylaid him under the mistletoe and was quite embarrassed when the tell-tale hairs of my pink angora sweater clung to his tunic!

The ponds and ditches froze solid the winter of 1939/40 and I amazed my village friends by putting on my skates – which I had brought with me from London – and skating merrily on the shiny surfaces while they were reduced to sliding. When I wrote home about this and how the children had *staunt Bauklötze* (stared building blocks: an untranslatable German expression!) at my skill on skates, Mutti wrote back immediately: 'Don't take chances on ice that is not frozen hard enough and pronounced safe for skating. Foolhardiness is no substitute for bravery.' I continued to take my chances.

Mrs Manfield had let me help her grind the dried fruit and suet for the mince pies. She also made the traditional Christmas pudding. The food rationing, which the government had introduced, did not affect us very much. Sugar was in short supply, but we had more than the one egg a week the city folk had to put up with. They were forced to augment their ration with powdered eggs, that had to be mixed very carefully with water in order to achieve *ersatz* scrambled eggs.

Since we made our own butter, we got well above the weekly ration of four ounces.. We stretched our meagre meat ration with wild rabbits and pigeons which John shot very skilfully and Joey retrieved with equal skill. I used to get angry at John for bringing Joey back from his hunting expeditions wet and shivering. But he claimed that the dog loved it. He was right, for Joey was off like a shot whenever John whistled for him.

Ironically, John was the one who wrote in my autograph book:

> God help the little rabbit
> And never may it die.
> Keep it safe forever
> Safe from Lord Woolton's pie.

> (Lord Woolton was Minister of Food
> and in charge of rationing.)

At Christmas-time we sang many carols and songs at school, and prepared for the Christmas play, the story of Jesus' birth. When one of the teachers asked me if I wanted to represent Mary in the play, I thought long and hard about it. I reasoned that Mary was Jewish, so I felt justified in playing the part. In a letter to Günter, I explained my decision. He did not object. I made a dignified Virgin Mary, wearing a blue flannel bathrobe and an old lace curtain draped over my head.

The Manfields had a big holiday dinner on both Christmas Day and Boxing Day with duck, goose, or pork – if a neighbour had killed a pig – Christmas pudding, mince pies, and a large Christmas cake, crammed full with dried fruits and topped with a thick layer of marzipan under a glorious crust of thick white icing decorated with red and green sugar. Aunt Mary brought out her homemade wine for all the visitors who dropped by during the holidays. She had prepared the brew in large tubs in the summer by letting raisins or cowslips ferment with yeast and sugar. It tasted very pleasant and the alcoholic content was minimal.

According to custom, all the villagers went to church on Christmas morning. I was exempt, of course, being Jewish. In the summer, I was the envy of all the children, since, on Sundays and other Christian holidays, I could sit atop a haystack and watch my classmates parade to church. I did, however, join my two special village friends, Edna and Margaret, in carol singing. We marched across the snowy fields, wearing our Wellington boots, mufflers, and gloves, to serenade the neighbours. I had learnt a large repertoire of Christmas carols by ear since I could not read music. Even with my gloves on, I was able to accompany my friends' on my recorder. People gave us cookies and homemade wine and also small change which we gleefully divided up.

Another event at Christmas was a whist-drive held at the church hall. We played the 'progressive' version in which the winning partners move on to another table. The winning couple won a prize, as did the one with the lowest score. It was a lot of fun, and we enjoyed the refreshments that were served with it.

With the coming of spring, carpets of wild primroses appeared in the woods. I gathered small bouquets, surrounded them with a collar of green leaves, tied them with wool, and sent them to London in a shoebox packed with moist tissue paper. My friends in the city appreciated my thoughtfulness. After the primroses, came the bluebells which formed a sea of blue in the woods! Unfortunately, these flowers were less hardy and could not travel by mail. I also helped Mrs Manfield to pick cowslips to be made into the Christmas wine.

Late in March, Günter and Hans were shipped to France with the Pioneer Corps to dig ditches behind the British lines. In order to protect the men from being shot as German traitors – since they had not been granted British citizenship – they were given the privilege of changing their names. Nachemstein, Hans' surname, changed to Nash, and their friend Otto Tramer became known as Owen Tyrell. My brother, Günter Lehmann, chose the grand-sounding name: Gordon Douglas Leigh.

Luckily, his unit escaped the bloody evacuation of Dunkirk by a few days. They sailed from St. Malo in a coal ship. One of the officers from the Ordnance Corps gave Günter a gas cooker to take back to England. Since the Pioneer Corps was issued no guns, I suppose he felt he could carry it easily. Hans still remembers him dragging this heavy appliance around, but he can't recall what happened to it once they arrived in England. He does remember that all of them were black with coal dust. After a few nights in London, the unit was sent to the beaches at Westward-ho.

I wrote regularly to my parents and described my new life on the farm and the many activities I enjoyed. The letters were slow in reaching them since they were sent via Uncle Berthold in Amsterdam, prior to the occupation of Holland. I did not write of my longing to be with them again, to be loved and protected. I was reluctant to betray my hidden emotions; I kept them to myself.

In May I had my 14th birthday. Mutti wrote:

My beloved little *Backfisch* (teenager);
    You are at an important stage of your life, half child and half young lady, on her way to becoming a complete

woman. I wish you health and happiness, hope and confidence, only then can and will everything turn out well and we'll be together again one day. Set yourself a goal so you can help to build a future for all of us. I come empty-handed this time and have to rely on others, unknown to me, to make you happy with some small loving gifts. I hope they'll do this, but don't be sad if they don't. My thoughts are with you. I would have liked to bake a chocolate-filled torte for you, but you will have to be satisfied with the picture I cut out of the cookbook and pasted above.

Summer came and with it the many berries I loved to pick. In the back of the house grew raspberries, loganberries, and red and white currants which we baked into tarts and pies. I could supplement the meagre pocket money that Günter sent me by picking blackberries which grew wild in abundance around the hedges framing the fields. It was hazardous work. Once I was chased by an angry bull and had to make a hasty retreat by climbing the closest gate. I had to avoid stepping

16 The Birthday Cake that Mutti Sent

into the 'pancakes' (cowpats) and risked getting severely scratched on hands, arms, and legs by the thorny branches. It was worth it! The people who came to buy butter and eggs from the Manfields also bought my baskets of berries. Some of them came from nearby towns in Bedfordshire and Northamptonshire.

Amongst the town people who were regular customers were Mr and Mrs Whiting, who took a liking to me. No longer feeling so childless, they 'borrowed' me quite often from the Manfields and took me in their car to their comfortable home in Rushden, Northants, approximately 12 miles away. They spoiled me by taking me to films and restaurants, and gave me a good time.

Mrs Stringer was another of my adult friends. She lived with her husband up the lane across the road from the Manfields. He had lost a leg in the First World War and had established himself as the shoemaker for the village. As a hobby, he set shards from broken china and crockery into cement, and the whole garden was filled with colourful structures. Mrs Stringer was a 'lady', and considered herself somewhat superior to most of the farm wives. She spoke well, read poetry and played the piano. I spent many afternoons having tea with her. She served cucumber sandwiches, those minute, thinly sliced little tidbits that only the English can make. Sometimes we had Hovis brown bread spread with Marmite, or another British invention: 'Angels on Horseback' (sardines on toast). I sat next to her on the piano bench when she accompanied our singing on the old upright: 'At Dawning', 'Alice's Blue Gown', 'Love's Old Sweet Song', and many more. I loved her overweight old terrier called 'Julie', who sang along with us in a low whine.

Mr Stringer never joined us. They called him Chick. A youngish-looking man, he very much kept to himself. I saw him occasionally when I visited the cottage to see Sally (or

17 'Julie' and 'Julia'

Julia as she preferred to be called.) He would laboriously drag himself around on his crutches. Mrs Manfield seemed to think that he was in constant pain. In the village, it was rumoured that Mrs Stringer was having an affair with Mr Jones, who came around weekly to replace the wet batteries that serviced our wireless sets. She was not very popular with the villagers, since she didn't mix with them or join their church or ladies' groups.

One morning that summer, there was great excitement in the village: Chick Stringer was found with a gunshot wound in his head. He had committed suicide. His gun was found nearby. People gossiped and blamed his wife for his death. She was shunned by everybody except Mrs Manfield, who was kind to her. I continued to visit her, but she soon put the cottage up for sale and moved in with an uncle and aunt who ran a chicken farm in the vicinity. (She eventually married Mr

Jones and went to live in Rushden. The marriage only lasted a year or two, since he fell ill and died).

Life went on as usual in Swineshead, in spite of the war. One day, the news reached us that one of the young men from the village who served in the Navy, Reginald Taylor, had been killed in action. He had been a close friend of both John and Harold, and I went to school with his younger sister, Joyce. The village, along with the Taylor family, mourned for him.

At the end of the summer, I helped in the hayfields, but I much preferred to hang around the blacksmith's shop and watch him hammer the iron causing sparks to fly. The blacksmith was very appropriately named, Mr Tuffnail. He set up shop every other week in one of Mr Manfield's sheds. Everyone in the area brought their horses to him to be shod. My biggest thrill was to ride these big draught-horses back to the field. Their broad backs forced me to spread my legs wide, but the discomfort was worth it. Only once did I have a problem with these patient creatures, when another horse on the other side of the hedge started to trot and my mount followed suit. It took a lot of 'whoas' to make him stop.

By the end of 1940, the war had intensified, and almost every night the sky over London lit up. We listened to the 'wireless' regularly, not only to war bulletins but to other programmes as well. From this old-fashioned contraption running on batteries, I picked up Vera Lynn's popular songs, including her best-known hit: 'We'll Meet Again'. We were amused by the 'Itma Show', which made fun of Hitler and his crew and also tuned in to 'Lord Haw-Haw', the British traitor and propaganda monger who tried his best to undermine the war effort. Nobody took him seriously.

I found great satisfaction listening to the classical music that was broadcast from time to time. This offered me an opportunity to become acquainted with opera, too. I listened to 'La Bohème', which was broadcast from a London performance and my knitting needles clicked to the rhythm of the music. I

18 Merry Christmas, 1941

was knitting underwear for Günter. Believe it or not, I made an athletic shirt and a pair of briefs out of natural two-ply lamb's wool. It took forever, but it was very much appreciated. Günter also sent me his socks to darn, which I then returned by mail. One time, I wrote back to him: 'I am returning your socks, but I kept one pair back because they were too thin to mend. Take some of my money and buy yourself a new pair.'

I also spent a lot of time drawing. My favourite pastime was copying cartoons especially the Disney characters as well as sequences from comic books. I also made my own Christmas cards in which I sarcastically portrayed Hitler as Santa Claus, or 'Father Christmas', as they call him in England.

Time passed and I was getting closer to 15. I had outgrown the village school. Most students left at 14, and Miss Smith, who was still teaching in Swineshead, gave me individual work-books with answer sheets so that I could check myself. I also learned a lot of poetry – Shelley, Keats, Wordsworth. I memorized these poems, very often not knowing what some of the words meant. What on earth was 'The Elm Tree Bowl'? But the poems stuck in my mind, and to this day I can recite Rupert Brooke, Walter de La Mare, and – of course – my favourite, Alfred Noyes' 'The Highway Man'. It was good memory training.

In spite of that, my brother found my education sorely lacking, and he moved heaven and earth to get me placed into a secondary school. Mutti also wrote that she was concerned about my education. She knew I had many talents and should be given training to develop them in a field that would lead to a profession. Finally, Günter succeeded in persuading the Jewish Committee, which was my legal guardian, to send me to Bunce Court School, a boarding school in Shropshire.

I left Swineshead in February 1941.

4 • Essays from School

The following four essays described my life in Swineshead. They were written for Mr Wormleighton's English class at Bunce Court School in 1941. I was 14 years old.

A Day in the Village

'Time to get up!'

I sat up in bed with a start. Oh, that was only John, Mrs Manfield's youngest son, going to work. He usually called underneath my window to wake me up. Well, I had plenty of time because John went to work at 7.45 am.

I jumped out of bed, as it was my habit to get quickly out of the warmth of the blankets, and casually dressed myself. The day before, I had fetched a jug of water from the soft-water tub, and I was now going to use it. A cold wash is always very refreshing, and it wakes me up. After I had washed, cleaned my teeth, dressed and brushed my hair, I went down to breakfast. Mrs Manfield asked me what I would like, and I told her that I fancied a piece of toast. There was a lovely red fire, and it did not take me long to make a piece. While I was eating, the dog 'Joey' sat up and begged for a piece, while all three cats tried to climb on my lap. I soon put the cats down, except my kitten Topsy. I shared my breakfast with the cat and dog, because I dislike seeing them beg without giving them anything.

After breakfast, I gave all the cats their breakfast. I know they always enjoy their bread and milk because they eat it up in a very short while. Mrs Manfield had cleared the table in the meantime, and I started to wash up the dishes. I helped her till, looking at the clock, I saw that it was time to go to school. Hastily I brushed my shoes, put on my coat, took my gasmask, fountain pen and copybook and set off. I had only a very short way to walk and arrived there punctually at 9 o'clock.

Our teacher informed me that the infant-teacher was ill that day and asked me to teach the little ones as I was the oldest girl in the village school. I did not mind that at all. First I had to teach an arithmetic lesson. I gave them little sums, marked them and heard them say their multiplication tables. I nearly lost patience with one little boy. Then I heard them all read, and afterwards I let them write a few sentences. To end up I read them a simple history story. All the little children told me afterwards that I was a very good teacher, which made me very proud.

At 12 o'clock we all went home to dinner. I had just enough time to wash up after the meal, make my bed, tidy my room and hear part of the news on the wireless, when I had to go back to school again. The afternoon period lasted from 1.30 p.m. till 3.45 pm. Before going into the school, I went to the one and only shop in the village to buy some sweets. I enjoyed afternoon lessons as we had needlework and drawing. We had to draw an aconite.

After school it was tea-time and I hurried home, because tea is the meal I like best. I did not find anybody at home, so I had to lay the table, make the tea, and cut some bread and butter. When I had just finished, Mr and Mrs Manfield arrived and also Godfrey. Godfrey, like me, was evacuated to the Manfields. We did not wait for John, because he does not get home till 6 o'clock. Of course, the cats and dog were bothering me again.

It was still light after tea so I decided to take Joey for a walk. He was very pleased to come across the fields with me, looking for rabbits as we went along.

When it was beginning to get dusk, we returned home to a bright and cheerful fire. John had had his tea and I was just in time to dry the tea things. Then I picked up my knitting, but put it down again because I remembered that I had a letter to write. I dislike writing letters in the evening, because I have got to get close to the paraffin lamp to see. At last I finished and taking my knitting, sat down near the fire. There was a good programme on the 'wireless' and I asked permission to switch it on. I enjoyed listening to a show while at the same time doing my knitting. Mr Manfield and Godfrey were reading. Mrs Manfield was mending and John had gone out. Joey was sitting on Mr Manfield's lap and Topsy had jumped into mine when I sat down. We all sat there till 8.30 pm. when Mrs Manfield laid the supper. I had a piece of bread and cheese and drank a cup of cocoa. At 9 o'clock I heard the news and went to bed after wishing everybody good night. I soon went to sleep and was dreaming sweet dreams.

Harvesting

As I lived on a farm for over a year I have experienced many different harvests but I especially remember one haymaking time.

It was on a Saturday, and after doing my usual Saturday morning house-work I went up the field to help Mr Manfield with the haymaking. It was a very hot day. The sun was shining brightly from a cloudless, blue sky. I had to rake the hay together and pile it up in heaps so that Mr Manfield's son John, who came around with horse and cart, could pick it up. Not much was spoken. Everyone was busy with their work.

At about 12 o'clock, Mr Manfield said to me,'Go and run home and tell Mrs Manfield that she should send the dinner up to the field. We don't want to stop now, we are getting on so nicely.'

I ran back to the house, climbing over gates and squeezing through hedges, as that was the shortest way. When I got home, Mrs Manfield was just ready to put the food on the table. She did not seem very pleased when I gave her my message.

'Well, I suppose I will have to', she said. 'Let's pack it up.'

We put everything into a basket, a dish of potatoes, a dish of vegetables, some sliced meat, a pot of stewed fruit and custard, plates, knifes, forks, spoons and cups. Besides, I had to carry a can with tea, and Mrs Manfield brought a Yorkshire pudding in a tin. We were just ready to go when I suddenly remembered that our little dog was also up the field. We found a little space in the basket for a few biscuits and a bone. Also some apples found a place.

We decided to go the shortest way. It was an awfully difficult journey. I could quite imagine how people on an expedition must feel on a journey of discovery. Whenever there was a gate, one of us had to get over while the other one handed the things over the top or through a hole. We were quite exhausted when we got there, but the food was greeted with so much cheering that we had to laugh. John and one of the workmen fetched bundles of hay for seats and arranged them around an open space where we put the dishes and plates. It was a lovely meal. I don't think I have ever enjoyed eating in a restaurant as much as I enjoyed eating in the open field.

After dinner we all had a little rest in the fresh hay. Afterwards Mrs Manfield and I carried the things home again. This time the load was considerably lighter.

Tea was also brought to the men working in the field. They worked until it was getting dark. Then they came home for supper, and went to bed immediately, tired after a long day of harvesting.

Sunday in a Village

Sunday dawns over a little village. A cock crows and others join him. The farmer turns in his bed.

'It is Sunday' he thinks, and sleeps on. One after another the farm animals wake up. The dog barks because he wants to go out, and the cats mew for their breakfast, and the cows want to be milked and fed. On Sundays, the farmer's wife is the first one to get up. She lights the fire, puts the kettle on, and makes the morning cup of tea. She brings her husband a cup to his bed, eats her breakfast, and dresses for church. The bells for early communion service are ringing as she walks down the street. The dog accompanies her part of the way, and then runs back to wake his master. The farmer gets up and prepares breakfast for himself, cats, cows, chickens, and ducks. Then he milks the chewing cows. When his wife returns from the service, she does her usual housework while her husband takes a short walk around the fields.

Now the village gets more lively. The first cars and bicycles pass along the empty roads, and the dogs bark at every passing stranger. If one walks down the street one meets people in their Sunday clothes. One can hardly recognize the working men, who a day before had looked dirty, torn, and unshaven, but who now wear collars and ties, and are clean and neatly dressed. The children wear light summer dresses and straw hats. They are on their way to Sunday school. The parson stands outside the church, joking and playing with the smallest amongst them.

The village shop is closed, but people go to the back door and ask for chocolate or cigarettes. The shopkeeper's wife is too kindhearted to tell them that her shop is not open on Sundays.

At dinner time the village street empties and everything is quiet for a few hours. After a tasty Sunday dinner one wants a rest. The farmer and his wife sleep in their comfortable armchairs, the dog lies on the mat, and the cats roll lazily in the hot sunshine.

All are startled when a bus rumbles down the street. It stops at the public house, and is soon surrounded by children who want to see if any of their friends have come on the bus. It is time to prepare tea. If there are visitors there are special cakes. As soon as tea is finished, the church bells ring again. The parson has arrived in his little car. Most of the people go to church in the afternoon. The village boys ride by on their bicycles, smoking and chatting.

Then the people come out of the church. The men go straight home and the women collect in little groups to gossip. But one by one they also go home, and the streets are empty once more.

Now the farmer and his wife go for a little evening walk accompanied by their barking and yapping dog. The farmer is smoking his pipe. The sun is setting behind the woods and the air is clear and cool. When they get too cold they go home to sit in their armchairs by the fire. She knits and he reads. The dog is on his master's lap, and the cats sit on the mat. Soon they shut the animals up and the farmer makes his round, to see if everything is all right. His wife locks the doors and then they go to bed.

The village is quiet except for a few late cars or cyclists who, having returned from a dance, picnic, or public house, go home singing and talking. Then everything is really quiet at last, and the moonlight floods the little village which is lying in a deep sleep.

The Village Blacksmith

Boom, boom, goes the hammer on the iron. Mr Tuffnail, the blacksmith is hard at work. He is a big man with mighty fists, wearing navy blue overalls and a dirty apron. His shirt sleeves are rolled up and show his big muscles as he hammers the iron. From time to time he holds the horseshoe into the fire again, pulling the rope which works the bellows to make the fire flare up. When the iron is red hot the hammering starts again and the sparks fly in all directions. Next to his workshop is a shed where the horses stomp the ground. Mr Tuffnail has now finished the horse shoe, and goes out to the horses. He pats them, lifts one of the legs and starts to nail the shoe to the horse's hoof, shouting, 'Steady, boy!' when it moves or kicks.

The first horse is now finished, and he turns to a beautiful chestnut mare. She is very spirited, and Mr Tuffnail has a hard job to lift her foot, loosen her shoe, and trim her hoof into shape.

Then the same process starts again. He holds the horse shoe into the fire, hammers it, and fastens it to the horse's hoof again. While he is hard at work, the owner of the horses comes back.

'Are they finished?' he asks.

'Not yet', is the answer. And then: 'This 'ere mare is a fine one, mister.'

'Yes, but a bit wild.'

And they talk about horses.

In the middle of their conversation, another farmer comes and brings a part of a plough which is broken. Others come and bring more horses which are to be shod. Mr Tuffnail is busy today. He has now finished the spirited mare, and her owner takes her and his other horse away. Outside the yard some children are waiting.

'Please, may we ride her home?' they ask. The good-natured farmer lifts two of them onto each horse, and the happy children laugh and shout.

Mr Tuffnail works until late in the afternoon. Then he goes home to have a good wash and a well-deserved cup of tea.

5 • Bunce Court

Armed with loving wishes for good luck and success, amply
supplied with provisions, and warmly dressed in my brown
tweed coat, I took leave of Swineshead. My loving mother,
with my growth in mind, had bought the coat before I left
home. True, it looked a little worn, the mouton collar shabby
and dull, the belt frayed, but it still fitted me, if a bit snugly.
The length was at last just right. Anyway it kept me warm on
that cold, damp February day.

I travelled to Bunce Court by bus and train, was met at the
station by two staff members and driven to the school. They
immediately ushered me into Anna Essinger's room. I felt
shy and intimidated facing this large, imposing woman,
with thick owl-like glasses. Her bulk completely filled her
capacious easy chair. Her brown hair, streaked with grey, was
pulled back into a bun. 'Tante Anna' or T.A., as she was called
by everyone, was the moving force behind Bunce Court, pre-
siding with complete authority. She greeted me kindly. Her
English had a slight un-British inflection.

I found myself in a room that doubled as her bedroom,
office and study – holding not only a couch which served as a
bed, lavishly draped with a flowing cover and strewn with an
abundance of pillows – but also her desk and the easy chair
she now occupied. It was a cosy room, warm and protective.
A well-tended fire burned in the grate. Above the mantel
hung a large reproduction of Michelangelo's 'Creation of
Man'. This great piece of art made a lasting impression on me.
I had never seen it before. There was God, portrayed as a
kindly old man, lovingly extending a finger to a naked human

left to fend for himself. Many people had also extended a helping hand to me when I needed it. I could identify with that.

Anna Essinger, one of the outstanding pioneers of progressive education, was born in 1879 of Jewish parents in Ulm, not far from Munich, the oldest of nine children. Her early education was in Ulm, but at the age of 20, she went to study in the United States where she gained a teaching degree. From 1904 until 1918 she taught at the University of Michigan and also administered a student residence. While in America, she became interested in the Quakers. Their beliefs and charitable work appealed to her, and upon returning to Germany, after the First World War, the young Anna Essinger worked for the organization setting up soup kitchens and places of refuge for needy women and children.

She was a critical observer of the German school system where the rod was not spared. As in many European schools, especially in the lower grades, children were taught by rote. They were not allowed to question the teachers, and – above all – were forced to adhere to a strict code of behaviour. Everyone rose when the teacher entered, sat at command, raised their hand when ready to answer and stood up when being addressed. All adults were greeted with handshakes, girls curtsied and boys bowed. Just as it was commonly said: Children should be seen but not heard.

Anna Essinger had other ideas. She was interested in liberating children from this rigid regime. They had rights to express themselves, to question, and above all to be creative and productive. With this credo she founded her own school in May 1926, Landschulheim Herrlingen near Ulm. She also involved three of her sisters: Kläre, Bertha, and Paula in this project. Here she would give the students an education that stressed self-discipline and self-help along with the subject matter. She, as well as other advocates of progressive education, instituted new areas of study such as Nature Study,

Humanities, and Psychology as well as practical skills like sewing and woodworking, which became part of the curriculum.

Every child contributed to the running of the school by helping with the housekeeping chores, food preparation, or general repairs. In this way all students as well as staff members had equal responsibility for the functioning and well-being of the community. This also helped to keep the costs down. A sizeable vegetable garden was tended by the children and supplied the whole school with fresh produce.

In April 1933, after Hitler came to power, Anna Essinger was ordered to fly the Nazi flag in honour of Hitler's birthday. She refused. Rather than face questions on this matter, she sent the whole school on an outing into the countryside. Shortly after this incident, Anna Essinger decided that Germany was not a place where children could grow up in honesty and freedom, and she made plans to establish the school in another country. After exploring possibilities in Switzerland as well as Holland, Anna Essinger went to England. There she found not only sympathetic supporters of her ideas but also a stately residence, Bunce Court, with several acres, a garden and wooded area, which seemed suitable for her purpose. It was located in Ottenden, Kent, not far from the East coast. In October 1933, the school, with 71 students and 16 staff members, including her sisters Bertha and Paula, was transferred to Bunce Court.

Bertha was the housemother, in charge of housekeeping, while Paula took care of the infirmary. The buildings were in poor condition and everybody including teachers set about the task of cleaning, renovating, and furnishing the school. The boys even made chairs and tables in the woodworking shop. Soon the school became known for its progressive curriculum which was patterned on the German *Real Gymnasium*, but conformed to an independent British boarding school.

In late 1938, after *Kristallnacht*, and throughout 1939, close to 10,000 Jewish refugee children came by *Kindertransport* to England and many were settled at Dovercourt – a summer campsite not far from Bunce Court – on a temporary basis. This was hastily prepared to accommodate these unaccompanied children.

While Anna Essinger was not a Zionist and had no particular interest in organized religion, she agreed, at Dr Norman Bentwich's request, to take charge of the children. Dr Bentwich was a Zionist, lawyer, scholar, and a prolific author. Formerly, he had held the post of Attorney General in the Mandate Government in Palestine. Between 1933 and 1936, he served as director of the League of Nations' Commission for Jewish Refugees from Germany. With the assistance of some staff members and older pupils, Anna Essinger organized activities and studies, as well as helping with the food distribution. She took a large number of these refugee children to Bunce Court, mostly older ones whom she selected personally because she felt they would fit in and younger ones because they were more adaptable and could grow in her school. The little ones were housed in a separate cottage with a supervising staff. The facilities soon overflowed and some children had to be accommodated at a nearby hospital, while other youngsters were given living space in a large farmhouse in the area.

The financing of the school was an ongoing problem and Anna Essinger depended heavily on contributions by private benefactors as well as the Jewish Committee and Quaker organizations. Many a day she would go up to London to solicit funds.

With the outbreak of war, foreigners were no longer permitted to reside in the coastal towns of England for security reasons. Most of the male teaching staff was interned, as well as boys over 16. A new site for the school had to be found, and Trench Hall, in Shropshire, was the selected place. It was an impressively solid mansion on top of a hill, overlooking the countryside with wooded grounds, gardens, and a large lawn. Early in 1940 the whole school was moved there. This was the place I came to that early evening in February 1941 at the age of fourteen.

After meeting my future roommates, I was assigned a bed, the bottom of an iron bunk which had been occupied by a girl who had contracted whooping cough. She was consequently moved to a billet in the nearby village of Wem so the disease should not spread. Unfortunately for me, it did. Although I had not even met the unlucky girl, some of her germs had lingered on and I became a victim! Here I was in a new situation, hardly acclimatized, feeling very much an outsider in the close-knit community at the school and then promptly sent to stay with an elderly lady in the village. I felt like an outcast. Once in a while, a staff member would bring me my mail, some books to read, and get-well notes from the room-mates I hardly knew. On occasion the local doctor arrived on the scene, tapped me here and there and proclaimed that there was nothing he could do. Neither the cough medicine nor the food stayed down with my coughing, whooping, and retching.

Like all things, it eventually passed, I was pronounced no longer infectious and allowed to join my fellow schoolmates. However, a slight cough accompanied by whooping remained with me for another few months. Actually, all the students stayed pretty healthy in spite of inadequate heating. The worst ailment was chilblains, which mainly affected hands and feet – especially heels and ankles. They not only itched to distraction but in some cases cracked the skin and became very painful. It's a typical English ailment, born of cold and dampness.

I settled down at school and adjusted to students, teachers, and schedules. As the main building was not large enough to accommodate the 100 or so students and 30 odd staff members, every available space was converted into living quarters. The former stables became dorms for the boys, while tack rooms, pantries, and smoke rooms were transformed into staff housing. The girls were assigned to the lovely large bedrooms with views of the rolling fields. Six or seven iron bunk beds as well as some chests-of-drawers, were placed against the wall .

All the rooms had names: The International Room, The Music Room, The Foxhole, The Saddler's Shop, etc. I was assigned to the International Room, shared by ten or so girls. Downstairs on the main floor were several spacious rooms furnished with long wooden tables and benches. These were classrooms, which quickly converted to dining rooms at mealtimes.

T.A. always joined everybody for lunch and dinner, while taking breakfast and tea in her room. The students took turns bringing T.A. her breakfast or tea tray and ran errands for her. Often she asked for a particular student to whom she might want to speak on some matter or other. There were many who preferred not to go into T.A.'s room unless summoned. They felt her presence overpowering and intimidating, as I did at our first meeting.

The tables were assigned to adults, and our names were listed under theirs on seating charts that were posted weekly. Whoever made up these lists saw to it that there was a mixed group, younger children with older ones, gregarious ones with quiet, shy ones, and more popular students with those who were generally ignored. We knew that at T.A.'s table the conversation was intellectual and slightly subdued, whereas other tables were more boisterous.

Our meals were served family style. Two of the table members were selected to do 'table-duties' for the week and had to collect the food from the kitchen as well as clear the table. This task had a special bonus. Instead of returning the left-overs to the kitchen, one could make them disappear on the way to the pantry or use one's fingers to clean the dessert bowls outside in the hallway.

As soon as the platters and serving dishes were set down, we all stood up in place, linked hands at the sound of the gong, and observed a minute's silence. This lovely custom must have been copied from the Quakers. It not only served as a silent prayer of thanks, but calmed the rambunctious and fostered an awareness of one's neighbour. If you missed the gong, you were late for the meal.

Apart from doing 'table-duty' we were assigned to other chores. A very popular assignment was 'kitchen-duty'. Not everybody was chosen for this hard work. You had to be selected by our very outspoken and highly respected cook, Gretel Heidl, nicknamed 'Heidsche'. This duty entailed getting up at the crack of dawn on Saturdays and Sundays and working until after dinner for those two days. But it also meant being privileged to eat with the staff in the kitchen, picking and choosing your food, and having more than one helping of dessert plus getting to lick the huge bowls in which it was prepared. Many of the sweets were made with real whipped cream, which we laboriously beat with a wire whisk for what seemed hours.

The huge iron pots used for cooking were heavy to lift and messy to clean, but you worked hard so as not to incur Heidsche's wrath when things were not squeaky clean. You avoided crossing her at any cost. Her raised voice with its heavy Swabian accent was awesome and you were at risk of losing the privilege of kitchen duty. One of the kitchen chores was preparing the English breakfast mainstay: porridge. The oatmeal was cooked in a huge pot in the evening, which Heidsche lifted with bulging muscles into a wooden box, covering it with quilted pads and laying it to rest until the next morning. It turned into a brownish glue-like consistency. Some liked it with sugar or honey, but it never appealed to me.

Off duty, Heidsche was a charming lady who liked to laugh and joke. The greatest treat of all was being invited to her little room adjoining the kitchen for an evening of coffee, cake, and conversation. I felt privileged to be one of this little group.

Every Friday, a list was posted for cleaning duties. All the rooms were thoroughly gone over weekly. Three of us had the responsibility to mop, wax, and polish one of them. It was customary to pair off couples or friends this way, and you could always tell from these listings who was attached to whom for that week. Of course, sometimes our thoughtful organizer of cleaning-lists was not up-to-date and we had to swap with somebody else. It was a hard job, especially since the polishing of the floor was done with what we called a 'blocker', a heavy block of iron – padded, of course – attached to a metal handle which was pushed in straight lines along the floorboards. We rushed to finish, because Friday evening was always special. There was a run for the few bathrooms. The girls dressed up in their best clothes and helped each other with their hair. We also swapped and borrowed clothing. The rooms and halls smelled of floor polish and cleanliness.

Besides having a short religious service for those who wanted to attend, there was always a concert. Often a performance by our talented music teacher, Lotte K., who was a very accomplished violinist and vocalist, or by Renate, one of the cooks, who played the viola, or a combination of capable students and faculty members. At the conclusion of these recitals, we would sit in silence for a minute or two and then leave quietly, a custom very foreign to the present concert-goers, who will often applaud wildly even before the last note is sounded. If there is no applause, you leave immersed in the music, the beauty of the sound still in your head.

Also on the staff was Mr Katz, a musician who played the recorder. He soon had everybody organized into groups and endlessly composed rounds and canons for the instrument, which he presented to his students on the backs of postcards dedicated to them on their birthdays. I was also presented with one, although I was not enamoured of the recorder and its limitations. Mr K. was not a popular teacher. We often made fun of him. His wife, a physician, was generally liked, but we were very sceptical about her medical practice of submerging us in hot water for whatever ailed us, and then dousing us with cold water immediately afterwards. Whatever the value of this treatment, we all survived.

Miss Hanna Bergas was our housemother as well as our French teacher. She was assigned a tiny room between T.A.'s large bedroom-study and the girls' bedrooms on the other side of the hall. We called her affectionately 'Habe' (H.B.). A highly educated woman, strict but kind, she taught us well. Physically she was extremely thin and flat-chested with a large nose and black hair peppered with grey, which escaped her bun in little ringlets. There was something heron-like about her which lent itself to caricature. H.B. had a close relationship with her cousin, Mr Schneider (or Schneiderlein, as he was called). He was unquestionably the most popular teacher at Bunce Court. He was not only extremely artistic, but he was gentle, even-tempered, and cheerful. He taught us art. Schneiderlein was also a good pianist and had a pleasant singing voice. H.B. and Schneiderlein were devoted to each other and you seldom saw one without the other. Both of them were German but spoke English most of the time.

We spoke a mixture of English and German amongst ourselves. Most of the children at Bunce Court were of German origin, with a few Austrians and Czechs. Nearly all of them had left home without parents as I had, while a few had families in England. Others managed to emigrate to the United States, Shanghai, or South America before the outbreak of the war, waiting to be reunited with their children after the war.

The Jewish Committee in London contributed to my school fees. My brother also helped out. I didn't worry about the question of my keep. The students at school never discussed the fees, and very rarely talked about their families or their separation from parents and home. It was a painful subject that we did not care to discuss although the close knit community we found ourselves in gave us support and companionship and kept us occupied with endless activities. It was an island in the storm, not only isolated from other habitats, but like a large family with many members who were either loved and admired, hated and shunned, or simply ignored. There must have been some children who suffered from the separation and depended on the staff or older students to console them.

That first year of school, I received very few letters from home. My parents knew I was at a boarding school and had been informed about my illness and recovery. They both urged me to study hard and to make something of myself. We were told at school that the war organization of the Red Cross allowed personal messages of 25 words or less to be sent to Germany. These came back two or three months later with an equally brief answer. I received three communications telling me that Vati and Mutti were all right, although Mutti said in the June message that Vati was very emaciated. At least it was some news from my loved ones.

There was no contact with other schools and other students, and we developed a certain snobbishness. We considered ourselves more sophisticated than, and intellectually superior to, the British school population. Our education, especially in the arts and humanities was very well rounded, whereas in the sciences we lacked Chemistry and Physics labs and were only taught Mathematics and Biology. Our Mathematics teacher, Mr Lucas, was a boyish good-looking young man with a ruddy complexion, who played the cello with great seriousness. He had a tough time cramming Algebra and Geometry into us. We needed it to pass the school certificate, the final examination prescribed by the universities. If you excelled in this, you were exempted from the Matriculation Exam, which the universities required for entrance.

Mr Lucas, or Douglas, was one of the two British teachers who taught us. The other was our English teacher, Wormy – short for Mr Wormleighton. We liked his curly hair and beard, his tweedy, sporty look and his wonderful clipped English speech. He loaded us down with work. Every week we had to write an essay for him. Wormy liked my essays. I was able to express myself in English better than most in my class. My first essays centred on my experiences in the village. Later I wrote imaginary stories and fairy tales. I was told that I had a gift for writing.

Wormy also gave us long vocabulary lists which we had to study. It was very good training; these words remained impressed on my memory forever. Before a test we would split up into pairs; one would call out a word at random and the other would supply the meaning, or vice versa. Then we would switch places. The tests consisted of 100 given words or meanings. I learned my English well. My German, however, was slightly rusty since I had not spoken it for at least 18 months. Before long, however, it came back to me. Soon I was bilingual as were the other children at school.

As I was always interested in sewing, I took advantage of our very gifted teacher, Frau Wagner, who taught me the art of draughting patterns. With the aid of these personalized patterns I was able to cut out and sew a blouse for myself and later a dress. I spent many hours at the Singer treadle machine sewing clothes. The sewing room was Frau Baer's domain. She took care of all the mending that had to be done for the school and sat all day patching torn bed linen, kitchen towels, and aprons. Everything was salvaged and reused.

One of our teachers – whom we called Saxo, short for Mr Isaaksohn – taught us History. He started each lesson speaking in English, but lapsed into German as he proceeded. He drew a graphic picture of the French Revolution in two

languages by giving us a dramatic presentation of the up-
rising, the intrigue, and the heads rolling from the guillotine.
Like Madame de Farge, I knitted, not publicly but unobtru-
sively under the table. Some teachers would let us knit in
class. Most did not approve, but not many noticed that some
girls had developed a technique of listening attentively while
our hands were busy in our laps. We also knitted or read with
a flashlight under the covers after lights-out.

These were my reading years. I devoured all the books that
were passed around among us: *Anna Karenina, The Story of San
Michele, The Brothers Karamazov, Gone with the Wind*, Albert
Schweitzer's *Experiences in Africa*, and many more. Somehow
we found time to finish the lengthy volumes in spite of loads
of homework.

In the evenings we participated in study groups, seminars,
or choir practice. I enjoyed the discussions on art history,
literature or music more than those on politics or current
events.

I soaked up knowledge like a sponge and grew and
developed in many ways. My reading helped me to form
opinions and express them. I soon felt on a par with the other
students, some of whom had been at Bunce Court for a few
years. I made friends and integrated into the community. T.A.
must have liked me, as I was allowed to bring her breakfast.
Not everybody was chosen for that honour.

My best friend was Renée M. I thought she was beautiful,
with thick dark hair, a flashing smile, and a lovely figure. The
girls thought her very sophisticated, enjoyed her explosive
laughter and admired her stylish clothes. Renée and her
brother Frank, a year younger, had emigrated from Germany
with both parents who lived in a small flat near Paddington
Station in London. Renée had many admirers, and after
'lights-out' we shared confidences. We occupied the same
bunk bed, and every time the sheets were changed, we
changed our position, up or down.

For two short months Renée and I kept a common diary. In it we duly noted all the romances of our fellow students on the first page with comments such as: How long? – scared of each other – daily walks – dumb and smitten – or, in our own case – no comment necessary. We took turns in making entries about our observations and criticized the other girls. Nothing escaped us. We knew all the gossip, but of course were above that. We gave an account of nightly walks with the boys where cigarettes made the rounds and noted down other escapades.

In November 1942, I made the following entry in German:

Last night the boys of the Saddler's Shoppe played a trick on the girls in the International Room. After lights-out, the boys climbed on their balcony and lugged up a blackboard on which they had drawn a ghostly skeleton with phosphorus. This they accompanied with scary music. Mrs Baer, thinking it was a gas alarm, came storming into the room. She put on the light to ascertain that *Die Buberl* (Swabian dialect for boys) were not in the room (maybe under the beds?) The adults who had been summoned by the commotion had to calm the shaking and babbling Mrs Baer. The whole house was in an uproar. When things quieted down again, the boys met Renée and me in the library to report to us. The whole thing had gone according to plan. Unfortunately, they had set several fires in the Saddler's Shoppe in the process of using the phosphorus. It had not been serious.

My greatest pleasure was the drama group. Renée's brother Frank, at 14, was a very talented playwright as well as cartoonist. He wrote and organized skits and playlets, directed them and acted in them, too. I became very involved with this 'In' group and had a part in every play. One of these skits was entitled 'How People Imagine Heaven', and it portrayed different characters looking for an ideal place, where all their dreams would be realized. One was a schoolgirl who came to a heaven full of candy and ice cream, no school, no work, only fun and games. Other characters also had their secret dreams fulfilled.

In addition, we presented more substantial plays such as *The Merchant of Venice, Egmont* and *Lady Precious Stream* under the guidance of a teacher. At one point a professional *régisseur* entered the scene, a Mr Markwald. He and his wife had been interned on the Isle of Man, as had countless other 'Enemy Aliens', people with German passports. As the school was able to guarantee them employment, they were released. Mr Markwald worked in the garden and his wife, Pilar, helped out in the kitchen. This 'gardener' had directed plays and films in Spain where he had met his wife, a petite, delicate, dark-haired and dark-eyed Spanish actress. We benefited tremendously from his teaching and guidance. After he left Bunce Court School, he became part of the London theatre scene and went on to coach the famous actress, Joan Plowright, wife of the late Sir Laurence Olivier. Frank M would also go on to make a name for himself by writing a popular play, *The Killing of Sister George,* which was made into a movie. Amongst the graduates from the school were writers, musicians, film-makers, artists, and politicians, many quite well known. The rest of us, although achieving no fame, took away feelings of community, a good education, and fond memories which we applied to our lives as housewives, business people, teachers, and parents.

Günter came to visit me at school only once or twice when his leave allowed. I was longing to see him more often. The girls admired my handsome soldier-brother with his curly dark hair and jaunty moustache. He took me and some of my friends to the tearoom in nearby Wem where we could eat dainty little pastries, fruit tarts, biscuits, scones and fancy cakes filled with cream and custard, topped with heavy icing – treats we were certainly not served at school.

We were always hungry. Not that we didn't get enough well balanced food, but just the idea of being regimented by three meals a day with few snacks and no potato chips, candy, or other goodies was enough to drive us to consume all kinds of odd tidbits. We often waylaid the bread delivery man and bought loaves of fresh bread which we devoured in privacy with a few chosen friends. We would often spread it with Marmite (the extract I had learned to eat while evacuated to Swineshead), mustard, or – if we were lucky – jam or canned butter sent in packages from America. If one of us received candy, we generously shared it by putting a portion on our roommates' bunk beds.

One day, one of Günter's fellow soldiers from the Pioneer Corps came by to see me. Jule Stern was blond, bespectacled, and on the pudgy side. He seemed to enjoy the informal community of Bunce Court, or else he was a lonely lost soul looking for a pleasant way to spend a few days of his leave. Could he have had some feelings for me? It never entered my mind, but I gladly accepted his present of a collection of handwritten poems in both German and English. Most were descriptions of the devastation of war, but there were limericks and love poems, too.

These poems were amongst his writings:

DESTROYED VILLAGE

Here, where men died, destruction reigns supreme.
Nothing stands upright but a charred beam,
Some shell-pierced walls, some girders torn and bent.
This is Death's Kingdom, life came to an end.

LIFESPAN

If you were born in Germany, my son,
You'll be a soldier right away.
You'll be lying in the cradle
Hands on the seams of your diaper.

And if you cry, my child, remember
'Heil Hitler' is your cry
And like a good German
Lift your right hand at this time.

You won't learn to walk, however,for
In Germany one only marches.
You will be trained to goosestep
In good old German tradition.

You'll go to school; what will you learn?
'Mein Kampf' and 'Horst Wessel's Song'
March on parade, hip, hip hurrah,
Never getting out of line.

You'll enter the Young Folk Youth, become a soldier
The drum has you in its spell.
And so you march, straight as an arrow
Into the Hitler Youth.

You serve faithfully, so you can become
An SS man later on.
You only need to be eighteen.
That can be easily done – but you are mistaken.

Before you have reached eighteen,
You froze to death in Russia
The only time that you are happy,
My son, since you were born.

(this poem was freely translated from the German by
   A. Fox)

IN MEMORY OF BETTER DAYS
Dark lies the lake.
Softly we float.
White gleams the wake
Cut by the boat.
Time and his chains
Have passed us by.
Nothing remains
But you and I.

I corresponded with Jule for a short while, but then he dropped out of my life. I don't know what happened to this sensitive young man.

Günter was stationed in South Wales in 1942. One day, in Newport, he slipped and tore a ligament in his ankle. The Army sent him to recover in a rehabilitation facility, a converted castle on the South Wales coast called Dunraven. He wore the grand uniform of the wounded soldiers: cornflower-blue trousers with drawstrings – like pyjamas – a jacket to match, a white shirt, and a red tie. In this get-up, he limped around, as though he were a war casualty, thoroughly enjoying his stay at this scenic ocean-front location. He must have been fancying the company of the ladies, because I received a letter telling me that he had met a Welsh schoolteacher and was in love. Her name was Constance, or Connie, for short. I was crushed. I did not want to share my brother with another woman.

In May of that year, I turned 16 and had to apply for a certificate of registration under the 1920 Aliens Order. I visited the nearest Police Station, located in Market Drayton, Shropshire, and was issued a grey book which had to be duly stamped by the Alien Registration Office of the local police, whenever I visited another town – both on arrival and departure. It also contained regulations for curfew hours between 10.30 pm and 6 am.

Soon after my birthday, T.A. asked me whether I was interested in continuing my education at Bunce Court and working towards a School Certificate or preferred to leave and take up a profession. I thought long and hard about it. Günter left it up to me to make up my own mind and assured me that he would be able to get financial help to keep me in school. The prospects for other training were not spelled out, and I could only look forward to working in someone's household and continuing my education at night. I decided to stay at Bunce Court for another year.

Günter wrote to me in June from Carmarthen where he was stationed. His letter sounded rather serious.

St. Davids Hall
Carmarthen
21st June 1942

My Dearest Annemarie;

Whenever we have been together – unfortunately through my being a soldier it wasn't too often – we have discussed your future plans. Because I have and will regard it as my highest duty to look after your well being. For nearly seven and a half years I have striven hard to make many things possible for you, not only that I gave this promise to Father and Mother, but also because I am loving you just as a brother loves his sister. Naturally my role wasn't an easy one – to be a brother – a friend and parents at the same time.

I am recollecting my thoughts. I admit that we didn't get on very well first when you came. I am not blaming you, many factors came into it – new home and different company – new land and language, too.

Then came the outbreak of war and your evacuation.

You had a happy time in Swineshead, but it wasn't the right thing. You were longing for work. Then Bunce Court; it was a very different life again but you did very well . . .

So you see, dearest, I am before an important step. You know that there are two different expressions of love – one comes from the parents to their children or from brother to his sister – and there is a different love – and about this one I want to talk to you.

You most definitely have noticed, that now since one year I am very much attached to one person – or let us call it by the right name, that I am in love with some-body. It is Constance. She has expressed all her love and friendship during this year – she has helped me in so many ways – so that we felt that our friendship should be a permanent one – for all our life – and we call it marriage.

Yes, I agree it may come as a 'happy shock' to you – but I wanted only to talk about it when everything was settled, and now it is. We are going to be engaged in a fortnight or three weeks and will marry on my next leave, about the middle of August. What do you say now?

I know for certain that you and Connie are and will be very good friends. I know that you like Connie an awful lot and that you never will feel as having lost a brother. No, on the contrary, we both will be there now as your best friends, and you can come to us with all your troubles and problems and you will find that we have the fullest understanding and sincere love for you.

I have written to you a long and sincere letter, which shall explain to you what is going on in my soul and heart. I know for certain that you will understand me and approve of my decision to build my own – yours and Connie's – and not to forget our beloved parents' happier future.

> With my most sincere love and many kisses,
> I am – always yours,
>
> Günter

My answer was very prompt:

> Trench Hall
> WEM
> Salop
> 23.6.42

My Dearest Günter,

You can't imagine how I felt when I read your letter today. I cried and laughed at the same time because I felt so happy. I really had expected this but as Mrs Loewenthal was so definitely thinking that you would not marry Constance I got the idea out of my head. I am sure you will be very happy together and it will be a much nicer feeling for you to have a home. Also I will have a home again and two to help me. I know that it will not make a difference to our love as I am sure you will share it between Constance and me. What will our parents say? I am sure they would like Constance and anyhow they might have expected it any day. They will then think of me and wonder when they hear the same news from me. It will also be much easier for them when they come over if you have settled in a home . . .

I know that we did not always get on very well together but it was because you did not know how to treat a girl of 13–14, and I was influenced by my surroundings and other facts. And it is quite natural that we have different opinions at times as we are so

different, but as I got older I got to understand you better
and we got on well together . . .

From your ever-loving little sister,

Miechen

A few days later, Connie's letter arrived.

5 Palace Road
Llandaff
Cardiff
2nd July 1942

My Dear Annemarie,

This letter is to greet you and welcome you warmly as
my future sister-in-law. We are already good friends,
although it has been mainly through correspondence,
and I am certain this bond will make us even firmer
friends. In fact I hope you will look upon me not merely
as a 'sister-in-law' but as a sister . . .

As you can imagine, I am very busy just now. You will
have heard of our little celebration which is to take place
on Saturday. I *do* wish you could be with us! . . .

Actually, I am having to write this in school, and so I
must ask you to forgive me not writing a very long letter.

I had an exacting task last weekend! I wrote to your
parents – Günter translated it – and then I had to copy it!
It was so strange. But I hope your language will one day
be as familiar to me as my own.

Goodbye now, my dear.
With much love,

Constance X X X

I was invited to Cardiff for my next school vacation, and I met
Connie as well as her family. I liked Connie, although I found
her to be a little older than I had thought and not as
glamorous as I had imagined. Her family lived in a comfort-

able house in Llandaff, a suburb of Cardiff. Connie's father was active in the church and played the organ, her mother was sickly and rested a lot.

Their wedding took place in Cardiff, August 13, 1942 at the Park Hotel. It was a civil ceremony, and we all had drinks at the hotel afterwards. Connie had a blue dress made with matching hat and shoes and carried a large bouquet of red carnations. I was very impressed and not a little jealous. I wore a navy blue plaid suit with a yellow blouse and white socks. I had put my hair in curlers for the occasion and parted it in the middle. Günter was in uniform as was Hans, his best man. Just before to Günter's wedding, Hans had married Eileen, a pretty petite brunette. Connie's letter as well as ours were forwarded to my parents via Tante Käthe in America. They responded with great joy a few months later after receiving an account of the wedding.

> My Dear Young Pair,
>
> What a surprise! I felt just like Mie, I didn't know whether to laugh or cry. May all your dreams and hopes come true! My God, Son, if only your parents could have been present! My Huschi-Puschi and long distance runner has been transformed into a responsible husband which is hard for me to visualize. Dear Constance, be a loving big sister to little Mie. In my thought I press all three of you to my heart.
>
> Your Marta

Vati added this time a typed note which was infinitely easier to read than his poor handwriting on the ultra thin air-mail paper he had used:

19 Günter's Wedding, August 1942

My Dear Newlyweds!
Your news reached us with the greatest joy. We rejoice that you two young people decided to join your lives even though you are so far away from us. We know that this step was taken after due thought and you feel responsibility towards each other. We hope wholeheartedly that all those directly and indirectly concerned will be blessed by this step. We expect to celebrate our 30th wedding anniversary this coming year. Maybe unforeseen circumstances will allow us the happiness to celebrate in the midst of our children.

In December they wrote again. This time the letters were forwarded via Sweden. Mutti wrote that she had a mental picture of Connie and also of me, now as 'an almost grown-up' young lady!

Does she still remember how we made doll clothes for Kätie and Peter and how she wrote her dearest wishes to the angels at Christmas time, which they so promptly answered? How well I could use such a connection now. Alas, how far this lies in the past, long, long ago.

This letter also contained the disturbing news that my father's three sisters had died suddenly of the same 'illness' as Günter's friend's mother, it was a coded message that indicated suicide. My parents were aware that they, too, could no longer hope to escape the inevitable deportation, or in my mother's words – they were preparing for a winter journey: 'Unfortunately, we are forced to take a *Kur* [cure: to take the waters] which I feel will not do us any good.'

They expected to be deported towards the end of December, although Vati still held out hope that they might escape their fate, Mutti thought that the 'sickness' was too far

105

advanced. I don't know if they were aware of what lay ahead. She added: 'You tell us to keep our heads up, but you see, that is just the difficulty. But I promise that we will try hard. After all I want to live to see Mie's wedding.' She signed it 'Your old Marta'. This was the first time that she had signed her letter in this way.

Vati added that he too was overjoyed to receive our letters that not only showed our joy of life but a love of being that they had not experienced for years. 'We have lost not only our children but many of our friends and relatives these last years.'

He also mentioned that the journey to take 'a cure', as a change of air ordered by the 'Doctors in charge' was unavoidable. The main thing was to survive these terrible times. 'Enough of this bitterness. You three enjoy life, your youth and hope for a lucky star which will unite all of us in the end.'

This was not the last letter they wrote, although they believed it would be. There was one more written by Mutti in even and steady, bold handwriting, telling us that their departure had unexpectedly been postponed and that they were able to spend the holidays with their friends:

> My dear Ones,
>
> You must surely wonder that I am writing to you again, but our journey has quite suddenly been postponed, and so I will use the time to chat with you again.
>
> We were very happy to celebrate the holidays in the circle of dear old friends, who offered everything to make things festive and comfortable for us. Consequently we were invited several times for dinner, and our old housefriend, cousin Lottchen and Aunt Hetty practically outdid themselves. Those were truly wonderful and peaceful days. We thought a lot about you, and imagined how it went with you. The young couple among their loved ones, and Miechen with all her

practical presents that she made herself. I really believe that she has sent us a guardian angel.

So the new year begins, better for us than we thought and how many wishes and hopes are connected with it! What transpired, was for us the most frightful that we ever lived through, only the gleam of light due to you, made it bearable.

Uncle Max's death shattered us, especially since he was so courageous, strong and full of hope. Now poor Edith is all alone in that dirty nest [the small town where she lived], hoping to hear from her son. It is very sad that one can't help her. In this manner we have lost many friends forever this last year. But when I think of you, I am happy again and I will not lose hope that one day fate will bring us together again. One must only make up one's mind, as our grandmother used to say, and I will do just that.

Otherwise we are well, Eugen happily so, as he will tell you himself. Two days before Christmas I had a stupid tooth problem with a front tooth. My gums were cut, drained and sewn up and for two days I ran around looking like an African savage, and my face was black and blue. Afterwards my face glowed like a colourprint for a few days, that also passed and the tooth was saved.

Now, my dear ones, now you have heard from us once again and I hope you will write again, if possible to Aunt Hetty, who will contact us. Continue to stay healthy and as happy as I wish for you to be, and think from time to time about us.

Your loving
Marta.

Vati added that he was glad to be able to write once more before their departure and that he was feeling much better physically than he had in the last few months. He also expressed the hope for a reunion in the near future.

That was their last letter presumably dated January, 1943.

In the summer of 1943, I sat for my school certificate at Bunce Court School, which I passed with flying colours, even earning a Cambridge Matriculation exemption. I knew that college was out of the question for me and when T.A. proposed that I go to Birmingham and be apprenticed to a Froebel Pre-school teacher, I rejected the offer. I told her that I really didn't like little children and had set my heart on fashion design. With that idea in mind, I bade farewell to Bunce Court and moved to Cardiff to live with my new sister-in-law. It seemed like a good idea at the time.

6 • Cardiff

I left Bunce Court with mixed feelings. It had been a safe haven, an island of fun and friendships, but, on the other hand, I had felt confined, shut off from the real world. I wanted to spread my wings, take my life into my own hands. After all, I was 17 now and ready for the world.

I liked Cardiff, especially the stately castle set amidst luscious green lawns and colourful gardens. It is believed that the Roman legions arrived at this site and established a fort as early as 54–68 A.D. during the reign of the Emperor Nero. A few years later, Wales was ruled by the Romans and the original fort was rebuilt. In the eleventh century, the Normans ruled and again built on the site of the castle. A succession of rulers followed, each adding towers and residences. But it was not until the latter part of the nineteenth century that the famous architect, William Burgess, was commissioned to restore the medieval structures. He also designed the wonderful animal wall which I loved so much. The solemn stone bears, lions, and tigers – as well as other animals – some with paws elegantly draped over the balustrade became like old friends to me. They seemed to recognize me when I passed them going to or coming from the centre of the city.

Connie's apartment at 47 Cathedral Road was not far from Cardiff Castle. It was a broad street lined with massive stone houses, four storeys high and separated by low iron or stone fences which enclosed the small gardens in the front of each house. Number 47 was converted into apartments, one on each floor. Connie's apartment was at the top, on the fourth floor. There were three small rooms, a living-room, two bedrooms, a kitchen and a bath. I had my own room. Connie taught music at a private girls' school in Cardiff. She had majored in piano and studied violin. Our love for music and our love for Günter were the only things we really had in common.

If I had been hoping for a sympathetic sister and confidante, I was disappointed. Connie did not fit the part. She was almost twice my age, being six years my brother's senior, and from another world as far as I was concerned. Reared in a churchgoing household with two sisters and two brothers, Connie was the middle girl. I found it hard to understand why Günter had chosen her for his wife. He admired her ability to play the piano very well, but I found her fairly plain-looking with her rather stocky build and high forehead, which she hid under curled bangs in the style of Mamie Eisenhower. Her straight blonde hair was caught in a rubber band at the back unless freshly permed and curled. It bothered me that Günter – whose previous girlfriends (at least the ones I had known) had been glamorous and sexy – had settled for Connie. In my teen-aged mind, I would not have been satis-fied with any choice. A movie star would have been criticized for other reasons.

As a housekeeper or cook, I could not compare Connie to my mother. She cooked English style, which – given the rationing – was difficult enough under the circumstances. I was fascinated by her perfect enunciation of the English language and watched her lips and rather large teeth very closely when she was talking. Was it her very Britishness that attracted Günter, her solid upbringing or her university degree? He addressed every letter to Connie with 'M.A.' after her name. Or was he looking for a way in which he could put down roots to become a part of the country he was serving? He tried at all times to conform to the English, and his musical ear made it easier to catch and imitate the subtle inflections in the language. Only the 'th' gave him trouble, as did the

English 'r' which is so different from the German pronunciation. He very rarely spoke German to me, nor did we talk about home or our parents. There was very little news of them.

Günter received a letter from Sweden that informed us that our parents had been deported to Theresienstadt in Czechoslovakia. We had no direct letters except one card that was received by Mrs Krenzisky, Hans' aunt in Stockholm, which stated that they had happily received news from us and were both well and employed. The very last personal card we had, was received in Sweden in November, 1944. It was dated September 16 and handwritten by Mutti:

> My dear ones, thank you for your detailed news. My thoughts are with you. Wish you further everything good, luck, and success. Am healthy and await further news. With love, Marta.

The return address was Theresienstadt – Protektorat Boehmen, Mähren, Bahnhofstrasse 3. It was stamped with the information that a reply was only permitted on a postcard written in German which had to be sent to the *Ältestenrat der Juden in Prag* (Elders of Jews in Prague). Vati was not mentioned on this card and Mrs Krenzisky remarked in her letter that he was probably not there anymore.

Soon after my arrival in Cardiff, I was apprenticed to a seamstress, Miss Litchfield, who was supposed to train me in the art of dressmaking. Instead she left me in a room by myself all day with odd jobs to do, such as ripping seams and sewing hems. The days were unbearably long. I counted every chime of the city hall tower clock; I sang to myself, recited poetry in my mind, and felt sorry for myself. My employment there lasted one week. In the meantime, still set on a career in dress design, I had enrolled at the Cardiff Technical College for evening classes in design and life drawing.

I enjoyed the Life Class with its often far from beautiful nude models, but the Design Class was a bore. It never occurred to me that accessories are an integral part of dressing, and I didn't care a hoot for hats and handbags. I switched my occupation to toy making. A friend of Connie's had persuaded me that due to the war, toys were at a premium and that I could make money by selling dolls from home. With a few yards of blackout material, some wool, curtain rings, buttons, and ribbons, I set to work producing little black Sambos with female companions for the British Christmas market. These dolls were ten inches tall with curly wool hair, curtain-ring earrings, button eyes, and colourful clothes; but the work was tedious and lonely and I could not manufacture enough to make more than pocket money. I listened to the radio or classical records all day. Connie had a large selection of the masters, and I became a very discriminating judge of recordings while my hands were busy sewing. Eventually, I could tell by the interpretation who the soloist was, which orchestra was playing and who was conducting. I felt I had to work somewhere where I would be with other people. During my years in school I had become accustomed to being in the company of young people at all times, and I missed that.

Connie and I scanned the wanted ads. My training was limited and there was no money to further my education. A clerical job at a large coal shipping company was about my speed. I went for an interview, passed an easy writing and maths test, and was hired by Paul Duffrin and Co. as a shipping clerk. Little did I know that I was not the only one with this title. There were at least six to eight girls in their teens who had the same task, namely to record the coal invoices into their ledgers. That was fine when the coal barges came in and we all scrambled for our particular invoices, but there were lulls and breaks – due to storms at sea or other delays – when there was simply nothing to do. I got tired of the girls' inane chatter about boy-friends, clothes and make-up, and I decided to increase my book knowledge. Along with my lunch, I always carried a book to work and soon finished works by Franz Kafka, Thomas Mann, Stefan Zweig, a Kurt Schuschnig biography, Pearl Buck, and many novels. I recorded all the titles in a notebook.

The job with the shipping company did not last either. Connie had a friend who worked in the Public Library, and through her influence, I was interviewed and hired as an assistant in the main branch in the centre of town. My boss in the lending department was Miss Daintree Duke. She was an elderly spinster, in her fifties, rather tall with a shapeless body. Her left arm was crippled and she had trouble using her left hand to remove the cards from the pockets that were found in the back of each book and insert them into the narrow envelopes which served as tickets for the borrowers. These were then filed alphabetically according to people's names. That was the system. Everyone who applied was entitled to three tickets except students who received five.

Miss Duke was considered a fixture at Cardiff Public Library. Her bright grey eyes saw everything and her iron-grey hair with its large bun would materialize out of nowhere. She took an instant liking to me, trying very hard to mother and guide me in a way she thought fitting and proper. For one thing, she would invite me to accompany her to church on Sunday, where she was a staunch member and also sang in the choir. Most Welsh people are musical and possess beautiful voices, and she was one of them. Needless to say, I declined.

People came in and out of the library all day long. The girls who worked with me were friendly, and we ate our lunch, gossiped, and did each other's hair in the staff room down-stairs in the bowels of the old stately building. I got to know many people who frequented the lending department, including Malcolm. He was a student at the University where he read philosophy and history. This young man would frequently bear a blood-red dahlia which he shyly handed to me. Attached to the stem was a slip of paper with a poem typed on it. The first letter of each line very cleverly spelled my name: Annemarie. Although I once chided him for misspelling it, I was flattered by his attention. However, I was really not attracted to this scholarly, rather short and stocky young man, who must have cared deeply. I am afraid I was not very attentive to him, although I was very much aware of his deep and liquid dark eyes which expressed devotion and loyalty. We played lawn tennis a few times, making up a foursome with one of his friends, Izzy, and a companion. We were not good at it, and it wasn't too much fun. I had no patience with Malcolm, and once got so frustrated that I kicked him, hence the reminder in one of his poems: 'To be a Lady'.

My wages were two pounds per week, which not only had to cover my car fare and lunches, but Günter insisted that I contribute to the household; so ten shillings a week went to Connie. Later I bought a bicycle and pedalled to work. Connie advanced the money for the three-speed bike and I had to repay her a few shillings every week from my salary. That didn't leave me much. I spent sixpence for lunch, which bought a good sandwich at Marks and Spencer's, even then known for their quality food. I could not afford to buy new clothes; besides, they were rationed. Many times I gave my coupons away to others who were more affluent.

I was making new friends. As I had always been interested in theatre at Bunce Court School, I joined the local drama club, 'The Cardiff Civil Defence Players'. At the time their production was 'The Rose without a Thorn', by Clifford Bax. It was the story of Catherine Howard at the court of Henry VIII. My role was that of lady-in-waiting at the court, and I fancied myself in the heavy flowing gown which was my costume. The best thing about the drama group was meeting Peter

Cardiff

Freundschaftsbund.

Accept from me this bond of friendship,
Nurtured in the midst of storm and stress,
Not weakened by those bursts of shameful fury,
Emitted oft in none too graceful manner,
Mistaking jest for jibe
And sincerity for provocation,
REmembering least of all,
Irrespective of one's years and nature, yet in appreciation,
Ever to remain a lady.

NEUJAHRSGEDANKEN, 5705.

Another year, no longer than a day,
Now drawing towards its solemn close,
Nearer brings the clarion call of victory,
Eagerly awaited by brave, enduring souls, yet
Moments devoutly prayed for still seem
A long way off, but radiant in their light,
Rendering hope and courage the more eternal
In every breast that heaves in constant faith,
Ever mindful of God's hidden ways.

Geständnis.

As reason must succumb before emotion,
Needing a heart pulsating with fire and flame,
Nor, when called forth, the power to explain
Affection in its most distracting form,
Many a fleeting hour slips quickly by,
Alas for concentration long since vanished!
Revealing, at the end, an empty page, yet,
I must confess, creation,
Evoked by ever constant thoughts of you.

Welsh, who played the Earl of Hertford. I fell head over heels
for this handsome young man with his dark curly hair, blue
eyes and small moustache. Peter was slight in build and very
animated. I found him to be highly intelligent and irresistible.
In his early twenties, he attended Cardiff University and was
interested in becoming involved in politics. Peter and I spent
many evenings walking and talking, and my adrenalin rose
whenever he rang the door bell.

Connie objected strenuously to my late hours, but I ignored
her protests. However, this affair was not destined to last. We
both decided that our love had no future. He came from a
large Catholic family. By mutual agreement, we broke up. I
was devastated, stopped eating and moped. Connie urged me
to get medical help but I never paid attention to anything she
suggested and we had many quarrels. She treated me as an
equal, not as a love-deprived child still looking for a mother. I
yearned for someone to comfort me when I was unhappy, to
heal the rift that I felt had opened between Günter and me by
Connie's presence. The mother-figure became more idealistic
than real to me. I wrote tear-stained letters to Mutti which I
buried at the bottom of my drawer. One of them survived.

Cardiff, 14.10.43

Oh Mother,

Why am I so unhappy when I have every reason to be
so happy? I love and appreciate my home. I love working
for it, sacrificing for it, but what I miss is affection. I try to
retrieve it, but I seem to do it in the wrong way. Nobody
can understand why I often act like a little girl. Why? –
because I, too, like other children would like to feel
secure, secure with you, on your lap with your arms
around me. And I am searching for this. I lost it too soon.
I believe that I can only find it with a man, this real
genuine love, where I can forget the world because it will
be all that matters. I would be all the world to him, just as

I have been to you, and I could return it. That is what I am longing for, and that is why I envy Günter. He has Constance, and she means everything to him, and being with her makes his struggles in life easier. It would make it easier for me, too, but as I can't have it, I must create it. I create it by changing my whole person and becoming another person. A person who fulfils all my ideals. But is it a good enough substitute? No, it wasn't so far, and I suppose it will have to be still longer, but now it is not enough anymore. It is too idealistic and too far from reality that it can no longer satisfy me. And this forever searching for a substitute for you makes me so unhappy and changes my views and opinions perhaps to a great extent. Perhaps this happiness and security will come one day either with you or with 'him'. I know I'll have to be patient and wait, wait . . . maybe forever . . . I don't believe in life's substitutions, but I do believe in life's balance.

Of course this letter was never mailed, but it helped to get my problems off my chest and commune with my beloved Mutti.

I also wrote to Günter. This letter was also buried in some drawer.

Cardiff
Thursday Night

My dearest Günter,

I thought I had to write to you, now in bed, as I feel utterly miserable. I have upset Connie again unintentionally. I know I did not do it on purpose, it was just that I was thoughtless again. I am beginning to believe that I must really have a bad character and I wish I could be far away as not to make you unhappy any longer. Now I feel regret, deep regret. I have apologized but that is all I can do. It is so much easier if you can just throw your arms around that person and say how sorry you are, but I could never do that, because I must tell you something that might hurt you. I can't ever love Constance. I can be on good terms, friends, companions, but there is always a distance. I feel most ungrateful because I appreciate all she does for me but I can't repay it with love. You see, parents expect to be repaid with love and are satisfied with it, but what can I give if I haven't got that? I have really tried my best since Sunday, but somehow there comes a slip and an icy barrier. As soon as I try to retrace something connected with 'zu Hause' [at home], I stumble and find myself crying about all lost things. I don't want to cry. I want to be like other girls. I don't want to feel out of everything but little incidents here always show me that I am a stranger in this country, the Englishman's way is not my way.

I know I am talking in riddles but I can't express what I feel. Please, don't show this letter to anybody.

I am kissing you in thoughts because I shall feel better then.

Your sister Annemarie

In the fall of 1943, I joined Habonim, a young Labour Zionist group. We met in a tiny room above the local synagogue on Sunday evenings, heard a lecture by our leader, sang Hebrew songs, and eventually joined the Sunday night dance below our meeting place in the Synagogue basement. This was run by the congregation for Jewish servicemen. The strains of the tango, 'Jealousy', had been drifting up to us already, and the girls no longer concentrated on Jewish History and the importance of emigration to Palestine and working on a Kibbutz. Downstairs, refreshments were served, and we tried our feet at the tango as well as the foxtrot. The boys in our group were less interested in the dancing. Two of them were very much into classical music. Cyril played the violin and eventually became a member of one of England's prestigious orchestras. Harold enjoyed listening to records. The two of us spent many hours sitting or lying on the carpet without the lights on, intently listening and comparing recordings of symphonies, concertos, overtures and other classics.

Whenever a live concert was presented in Cardiff, we joined the long queues which finally led to a cheap ticket in the back of the hall, or high up in the 'gods'. For very little money, we were able to hear the greatest musicians: Sir Thomas Beecham, Sir Malcolm Sargent, Sir Adrian Boult, Dame Myra Hess, Vladimir Horowitz, Yehudi Menuhin, Solomon, Benno Moseivich, and other greats who ventured to Cardiff in wartime for one-night performances.

We also frequented the old Cardiff Theatre, now long torn down, where the 'gods' were at a dizzying height in a cramped space under the roof. There we saw the late Shakespearean actor, Donald Wolfit, holding forth as Shylock, and we became familiar with the plays of Ibsen, J. B. Priestley, and Noel Coward.

The 'La Rosa Opera Company' came to town frequently. Though second-rate, I got acquainted with the most popular productions. I will never forget the rather hefty Madam Butterfly. When she knelt before the shrine of her ancestors, all the audience saw was a large white ball!

I met a very different group of people at the International Service Club, where I went with some girl-friends to mix with the soldiers, sailors, and Air Force men who came there on Saturday nights to drink, dance, and meet girls. We danced with everyone, including the black African men from the British Colonies. Most of them were well over six feet tall.

At that time, I also met some Indians who were studying in England. One, Kamlaker, was an engineer. His friend, Amahd, was interning at the Cardiff Royal Infirmary. There was also a young Indian woman, Lila, who was a physician and had settled amongst the Welsh miners, a short distance from Cardiff. She lived in an old, draughty house in a valley. She often entertained us there with home-cooked Indian cuisine which made me drink gallons of water to quench my thirst from the fiery curry dishes and to wash down the overly sweet desserts. After the meal we played recordings of Indian music and sat around talking. I was fascinated by their culture.

At the time, I was not aware of a colour bar in England. It was wartime, and many servicemen from the British colonies were stationed in England. Kamlaker was of dark complexion while Amahd was quite light. The British appeared unprejudiced, or so it seemed to me, until Connie mentioned the fact that the neighbours may not like a black man visiting the house.

Günter was still in the Army. He had transferred to the Royal Artillery and had been stationed at various locations in the country. He and Connie had bought a small house and we moved to this semi-detached home in the suburbs of Cardiff. In the spring, Connie had given birth to a red-headed baby, Peter. Kamlaker was crazy about the baby and asked if he could stop by to see him. He was crazy about me, too, engraved love poems on sheets of brass, brought me gifts and swore that he would make a good and faithful husband if I wanted to marry him. He made me a present of a sari and insisted that I have my picture taken in it. I declined his marriage proposal. I had no intention of committing myself to a life in central India, where his father worked on the railroad. Eventually, to my relief, he returned home to India.

The war was nearing its end. My brother was stationed in Ireland where he supervised German prisoners-of-war in a large camp. Many of them were very talented and transformed wooden crates into musical instruments, lamps, and other items. Günter brought home a lovely mandolin which

21 My 'Indian' Period

was playable and a lamp for the baby's room. He told us of one prisoner who had made a violin and was playing it. Günter had brought him the sheet music of Mendelssohn's Violin Concerto, which he had never heard before, as all music by Jewish composers had been destroyed by the Nazis.

Whenever Günter came on leave, I had to share him with Connie. After the baby arrived, I was asked to babysit Peter while the two went out. Günter always brought gifts of such unattainable items as silk stockings, leather gloves and perfume. The silk stockings and fine leather gloves were presents for Connie. As for me, I received lisle stockings and coarser heavily lined gloves, which he deemed more practical for someone my age. Hadn't he noticed that I was grown-up now? That I wanted to dress up for the boys? I was jealous of Connie and felt that she did not deserve this finery, since she did not go out much anyway while Günter was away.

At one point, he must have realized that I had grown into a woman, because he talked to me about being a flirt. 'Don't ever be a tease', he told me, 'men don't like women who tease.' I pretended to understand what he meant. My knowledge of sex was very sketchy. Most of it dated back to my school friends at the Jewish School in Berlin. The English girls never talked about the subject – at least, not to me. At Boarding School, we had discussed boys and girls together mainly in platonic terms and the relationships went no further than a kiss and touch. I had evolved the very Puritan view, that I had to save myself for true love. I was not confident enough to broach the subject to someone like Connie.

One of Günter's close friends in the Pioneer Corps, was Otto. He was Czech and had left his country in 1939 to seek employment and prepare a home for his wife and baby son. Unfortunately, they didn't make it out of Czechoslovakia. However, both of them survived in Theresienstadt and came to England soon after the war was over. Otto was a frequent visitor to our house. He was soft-spoken, warm, and fatherly, with a great sense of humour plus a fabulous gift for music. I grew very fond of him. Connie and Otto played Beethoven's Symphonies arranged for four hands on the piano. He was the one who first introduced me to the Royal Albert Hall in London, where he took me to hear a concert with Sir Adrian Boult conducting. I will never forget being almost jolted out of my seat by the brasses in Holst's 'Perfect Fool' ballet! Once in Cardiff, he sat down at the piano with me next to him and went through the whole score of Brahms' First Symphony.

While I lived in Cardiff, I spent a few weekends in London with my friends from school. I stayed with Renée and Frank's family near Paddington Station. We met with other old schoolmates, roamed London, and ate at ethnic restaurants. At that time, the bombings were few and far between and I was never forced to take refuge in an air raid shelter. Only once, in Cardiff, did I hear the whistle of a bomb screaming through the air, but the explosion was quite distant.

Other than my short trips to London, I took only one week's vacation in a Habonim Camp at Churton in North Wales. It was a working holiday. We lived in tents, cooked outside, and picked apples and pears for the nearby farmers. The money we earned was donated to Palestine. At this camp I met Steven Mendelsson. He had also come on the *Kindertransport,* and was growing up without family, lonely and without family guidance. We talked about the possibility of a life of farming on a kibbutz in Palestine and the founding of a Jewish State. Steven felt that he wanted to work for Zionist organizations. At camp that summer, we became a couple. In fact, he had a big fight with another boy who was vying for my attention. Steven won after beating up the other suitor. We used to walk and talk together, and stop for glasses of cider on the way. I taught him about music and told him that the plucking of the strings in the third movement of Tchaikovsky's Fourth Symphony was called 'pizzicato'. After the summer, Steve and I saw each other a few times. We wrote letters occasionally, but our lives took different turns and eventually we lost touch.

The war in Europe came to an end. On May 8 1945, VE Day was celebrated with dancing in the streets. If I thought that now I would be reunited with my parents, I was wrong. Slowly, the news of concentration camps reached us, but nobody realized that six million were lost. Günter contacted the Jewish Organizations to find out if there was any news of our parents, but it was too soon to locate the survivors and to compile the lists of the dead.

In September we received a letter from Sweden. Mrs K wrote that she had received a letter from a lady in Denmark who had been together with our mother in Theresienstadt and had since returned to Denmark. She related how Mutti had always been full of good humour and had a burning desire to be reunited with her children in the future. Unfortunately, she was deported from Theresienstadt to Auschwitz in October 1944, and there had been no news of her. Mrs K urged Günter to write to the World Jewish Congress in Sweden, as others had been traced. Günter wrote to Sweden as well as to the lady in Denmark. Her answer came promptly, written in English:

> I will tell you what I know . . . Theresienstadt was a concentration camp, but it was one of the best of them; there were no gas chambers. I came to Theresienstadt in October 1943. At that time, your parents were there. From the middle of November I worked in the washing establishment and delivered the clean clothes. Here I met your dear mother. She was in satisfactory condition and in good health and very optimistic. She told me a great deal about you and your sister and also showed me pictures of you both and your home in Berlin. About your father, I regret to tell you that he died in Theresienstadt. I don't know the exact date, but as far as

I remember it must have been between January and May of 1944. I understood from your mother that he was ill and that death came as a release.

Your mother and I worked together until September/ October 1944, when suddenly great *Arbeiter-transporte* [workers' transports] were sent from Theresienstadt and unfortunately your dear mother had to go. Your mother said, 'Then I will be nearer England. After the war, I go to London.' But unfortunately I have not heard a word from your mother. She had promised to write to me in Theresienstadt and she had my address in Copenhagen in the event that she should go to England via Denmark. Therefore, I have no hope that she is still living.

Sincerely,
Wilma Oppenheimer

I did not grieve. I could not grieve. I had lived as an orphan for six years. There was no funeral, no grave, no mourning relatives.

Life in Cardiff went on as before. The end of the war did not change our lives that much, except that the servicemen came home. It also brought an influx of a small group of 'Yanks' into the city. Over the last year, only a few had been visible. Either they were stationed in the area or had stopped in Cardiff on their way to nearby ports. A few Jewish soldiers from the U.S. had drifted into the Synagogue basement for the Sunday night dances, but not one American soldier had ever entered the Public Library lending department until that September. A lone 'Yank' appeared in the stacks and casually pulled a volume off the shelf. Overcome with curiosity, I grabbed some books to return to their places near where he stood absorbed in his reading and confronted him with a cheerful, 'Can I help you?' Yes, it turned out he was looking for Franz Kafka's works. 'In English or the original German?', I asked. 'Either', he replied casually. I found two books for him – *The Castle* and *The Trial*.

He was good-looking, of average height, slender with a nice smile and I was reluctant to leave in order to continue my job of replacing books on the shelves. He was loath to depart as well, and we remained standing together talking about Kafka in that hidden corner in the stacks behind the high bookcases. He promised to return the next day and he did – the next and the next and the next. His name was Frank Fox, and he had been sent to Cardiff with a group of 25 American soldiers who had been selected – because of previous college education – to take courses at various universities and technical colleges in Britain and France. My 'Yank', Frank, had chosen England and was shuffled off to Cardiff, where he signed up for basket-weaving or a similarly inane course which he never attended. He and his friend, Eddie Schmidt, a large, blond, jovial chemist from New York, were billeted with an elderly lady in Cardiff who was grateful for their ration cards. Left to their own devices, they would get up late and make their way to the library to fetch me for lunch. Frank usually spent the afternoons reading and waiting for me to finish work. Then he took me home.

Connie did not object to Frank, especially since he contributed to our 'high tea' by bringing us canned fruit, butter, chocolate and cookies. We often borrowed Connie's bike and rode all over the city and to nearby seaside towns. Frank's dark blond curly hair would fly in the wind, and cruising MPs yelled at him:

'Soldier, where is your hat?'

We went to dances, concerts, and parties especially arranged for the 25 college-attending Americans. In November, they celebrated Thanksgiving with turkey and all the trimmings. I was invited to the feast which was held in a hall at Cardiff Technical College. It was my first Thanksgiving.

22 Frank and I under Two Flags

After the meal we danced and danced, especially the waltz, which left us all alone twirling on the dance floor. We realized we were in love. Frank proposed to me, and I accepted.

When Günter came home on leave – not having been 'demobbed' yet – Frank approached him for his consent. My brother's question took him rather aback. 'Yes, of course, but can you support my sister in the style to which she has been accustomed?' Frank, all of 21 years old, assured him that he could, and we celebrated our engagement by throwing a party with all the American food we had hoarded. My friends came, although some of them were not sure which one from among my many boy-friends I was getting engaged to!

I had only known Frank a short time. His stay in Cardiff was coming to an end, and he was due to report back to his unit. Knowing that he had almost the required number of points to assure his passage home and get his discharge, we started collecting all the necessary papers to enable us to get married. The letter from his commanding officer stated that our marriage 'will not reflect unfavorably in any way on the U.S. Army.' Besides, we needed a blood test and I required a medical certificate confirming that I was in good health.

Since I was only 19, I required permission from the Jewish Committee in London – which was legally responsible for me – to marry at that age. The papers arrived, duly signed by Lord Gorrell. I had not known that a venerable Lord was my guardian. The way was now clear; we could go ahead with the marriage. Just one more thing was required: Frank's mother's consent. He had told me about his family in Philadelphia. His mother was a widow who lived with his sister in a small apartment. His father had died in Poland when he, Frank, was just 12 years old, and instead of going to Palestine as planned, the family had emigrated to America in 1937. His mother's two brothers and four of her sisters had preceded her there and could stand as guarantors for her and her children. One aunt was in business in Philadelphia and offered her sister employment. Frank went to live with this aunt and had completed his schooling at a prestigious high school in Philadelphia. Before the outbreak of war, he had worked at various small jobs while attending University classes at night. He assured me that the family would welcome me with open arms.

Frank and I had made the arrangements for the wedding ourselves. He bought me a stylish grey suit, an elegant fur coat of mole skin, a small rabbit-fur hat and a muff to match. Frank told me later that the funds for these extravagances came from the sale of a Leica camera which he had 'liberated' in Europe and sold to a Russian officer for a good price.

We made an appointment with the registrar of marriages at Cardiff City Hall for January 9, 1946. I quickly phoned one of my ex-boy-friends to be a witness, Frank bought a 'utility' gold band, and we were ready for our 'I do's'.

Günter could not get leave, but Connie joined us, and after the ceremony we had a drink at a nearby hotel. Then we left for London by train. With my big bouquet of red carnations clutched in my hand – Frank armed with a bottle of gin and a can of orange juice – with a wink and a knowing grin, the conductor ushered us into an empty compartment and locked the door.

We arrived in London, flushed and giddy. Two days later, a telegram reached us. It was from Frank's overprotective mother:

'Stop everything. Don't get married.'

7 • *War Bride*

A new life was starting for me. I was now a married woman, preparing to make a home for Frank and myself in a strange country. I was sure he wanted children as much as I did. It didn't matter that he had no job to go back to, or was not trained in any particular profession. He expressed an interest in journalism. I was prepared to work, and my employment in the library stood me in good stead, especially as I had qualified for a certificate from the Library Association while staying in Cardiff. We did not worry about the future, we had each other.

I brought no worldly goods into the marriage, except for some of my mother's linens which she had packed into the trunk she sent off after I left home. The few wedding gifts we had received from friends and all my clothes and possessions fitted comfortably into my old suitcase which I had carried from home seven years earlier.

I was glad to leave England. The war years had taken their toll. I was tired of rationing, blackouts and other inconveniences. The dream of being reunited with my parents, had been shattered. There was to be no dependence on a loving and caring family. Günter had his own family to care for. I had to be independent and stand on my own two feet. Of course I was no longer alone, I had Frank to love and support me. With these thoughts in mind, I arrived in London on the arm of my G.I.

London in January was bleak, damp and dismal, but not to us love-birds. Frank had decided that it was only proper and fitting that we spent the first night of our marriage at a hotel.

By an unfortunate coincidence, the United Nations had arranged for a major conference to be held in London at that time and there were no hotel rooms to be had for love or money. With Renée's help, we finally found a room in a seedy hotel in Bayswater. It was dingy and dusty, but it would do. The only thing wrong were the two beds, which were separated by a night table. No problem, however – we shoved and pushed until they were side by side. The next morning after a proper English breakfast, we moved to Renée's building.

Luckily for us, she had arranged for us to use the apartment belonging to her boy-friend, who was out of the country visiting his native Senegal. It was one floor below where she and her family lived in that tall apartment building, which is even now clearly visible from the train pulling into Paddington station. Frank and I were lucky to have the use of it, and use it we did!

I had left my job at the library knowing that I had to be closer to the American Embassy in Grosvenor Square and the British Home Office to check on my emigration status. I had no idea how long that would take, or where I was going to stay. After Renée's friend returned from his trip, the apartment was no longer available.

Frank commuted between London and Southampton carrying his army records with him. As far as the American Army was concerned, he did not exist. He discovered that others – with a similar length of service (or points) – were being shipped home. It would be best to wait around until he, too, was eligible. He hung around the USO and spent his time writing to me, reading and listening to records. He recounted all the plots of the books he had read and quoted the names of the records (78s) he had played. In a letter (one of the first of the 37 that followed) he complained about the poor condition of the recording machine:

. . . and now Schnabel (Artur) is playing the Emperor Concerto with the Chicago Symphony – very poor recording machine – the way it has Schnabel rush through this concerto you might think that he has to go somewhere – small wonder they've been playing boogie-woogie on it all day – even a machine has a heart.

Since there was no longer a place for me to stay in London, I travelled to Manchester where my old friends, the Loewenthals, had spent the war years. Frank wrote that he could not get a pass, apart from which he had no money. The girl working in the office at the army post was kind enough to let him use the phone whenever the boss was out. Money was a big problem for us at that time. I owed £20 to Connie's father and £7 5s to Connie on my dentist bill. I depended on Frank to send me dollars. Finally he collected his pay, but spent £4 on a portable Corona typewriter which someone had for sale. After all he was going to be a journalist! He was convinced that it was worth at least $75. The only problem was that it typed only capital letters. He sent it to me for safekeeping, and finally I brought it with me after dragging it around from place to place. Frank was expecting to board a ship to America any day.

On February 4, Frank wrote this letter from Southampton:

> The ship is the *Gustavus Victory*. If you have ever read a book by Frank Craven called the *Death Ship*, you will appreciate the comparison I am making. Not seeing you for two months will be painful. Each day will bring us closer together though, and before you know it we shall be walking down the main street in Philadelphia.

He closed his letter with the customary endearments that passed between us all along.

I wrote to him three days later.

My dearest,

I am thinking of you as the rain lashes against the window. My sweet, I hope you have a calm sea. How I wish, how I wish . . . I'll just keep on wishing. Your telephone call woke me up this morning, and you can't imagine how sleepy I was. It was rather trying to shout at each other when we felt like whispering the sweetest things. In spite of that I think I could have shouted: goodbye, for another five minutes just to hear you reply.

How I am looking forward to our new life! We'll share everything, sweetheart, fun and sorrow. Although you are so far away, I am not unhappy. I am happy in the thought that there is somebody who loves me waiting for me. I felt the same way regarding my parents. Otherwise I wouldn't have had much to live for. I used to talk to my mother just as I talk to you now when I am alone in bed and tell you so much more than the words I can put on paper.

Mrs Loewenthal enjoyed my company. We went to the movies together and I accompanied her on visits to her friends. One afternoon she took me to Stockport, a dull and dreary town, so grey that a bucket of paint spilled in the centre would be the only colour spot! My letter to Frank contained the following:

We ate lunch at the so-called best restaurant. Guess what? Sausage and greens, a coffee that tasted like washing-up water. The food situation is really serious. The papers are full of women's protest meetings all over the country. The people object quite rightly to being let down by the Ministry of Food, as they have made a lot of promises. Oh for the land where milk and honey flows . . .

I spent several weeks in Manchester, still waiting for news from the American authorities. I would be classified #2 in order of priorities, after supplying them with proof of Frank's arrival in the States. Besides, I had applied to the Home Office to issue me with a Certificate of Identity. So much red tape. I learned from the newspapers that the *Queen Mary* – back from delivering war brides – would soon be on her way with more. It wasn't my turn yet, although the paper also stated that the brides' dogs were being shipped at that time. I had to wait, however much I wished I was a dog.

I wrote to Mrs Stringer and she invited me to visit her at the poultry farm of the Shackletons, with whom she was staying. I complained to Frank that I felt like a wandering Jew. He had arrived in America on February 18 and gave this amusing account of his voyage:

Believe it or not, I spent the entire trip in the hospital. Was I sick? Certainly not. I worked there. But that is a long story. Ah, here is indeed a story worthy of a Fox. As soon as we boarded this pea shell I knew I shall not be comfortable. It was terribly crowded. There was so little room in the hold that the animals rubbed flanks constantly, developing all sorts of unpleasant odors. They had four-tiered bunks (of course I picked the top-most one. Old salts know that this is closest to the light, allows greater freedom of movement and is not subject to cascading regurgitations). But there was no hot water, no showers, no place to read, to contemplate. I slept there one night. I knew that something radical must be done . . .

Soon the sea got rough. Every animal got sick – it followed one everywhere like a raging flood. The mess hall, the bathroom, the quarters, the deck – there was no place to go. It may be funny when Rene Clair stages it, but this was entirely unrehearsed and quite messy.

Well, it was now or never. I naturally gravitated toward the wealthier part of the ship, the comfortable crew's quarters where the officers slept. I looked through the cabin windows and saw the clean sheets, the comfort and grew green with envy. My old hate for caste soon got the better of me . . . I always hate to see the officers eat their well-prepared food from clean, cloth-covered tables, with waiters dancing in attendance . . .

I walked towards the dispensary and hospital part of the ship. I suppose I walked there automatically. Well, on seeing the clean confines of the dispensary, I made up my mind. I walked into the dispensary. They were having a conference at that moment for they needed someone to give shots, as everyone on the staff was busy. There were two doctors and a few permanent personnel there to take care of the ever brisk business. They were saying: 'If we could only get someone . . .'

That was my cue. I walked up boldly and spoke surely: 'I can give shots.' The words fell upon them with the force of a descending boulder. I believe if they had needed someone at that time to perform a Caesarean, I would have told them I was capable of doing that too. Of course I had never used a syringe in my life, but I administered the first one that very minute and on the entire trip injected over 200 cc of penicillin.

It took me one day to master (ever so superficially) the pharmacopoeia (or however the hell that is spelled) and soon I was treating everything from fungicidal feet to gastro-intestinal disturbances. I helped set a number of broken limbs and was thereafter referred to as 'Doc'. Of course the rest is anti-climactic. A clean bed in the hospital, hot fresh water showers, ice cream twice a day.

When, O when, will fate catch up with this transgressor of laws, this perpetrator of abominable lies, this Fox? Not too soon I hope.

Frank's next letter was from Camp Kilmer, New Jersey. He had arrived in New York harbour very early in the morning on February 18 and watched the sun rise over the city. It was a welcome sight. He noted that not all the hanging gardens of Babylon could compare with the floating castles of Manhattan. Two patriotically decorated yachts came out to meet the boat – in spite of the morning chill – and two bundled-up girls sang impossible jazz songs accompanied by an amplified black ensemble playing on deck. After being served coffee and doughnuts by Red Cross girls, the returning soldiers were treated to a ferry ride around the harbour. Eventually they boarded a train to the camp where they were duly welcomed and fed. After two days of processing, Frank finally became a civilian again and headed back home to his family.

My stay at the chicken farm was short. Although I appreciated being well fed and having a double-yolk egg every morning (these were the eggs that could not be sold), I was no longer accustomed to living with the discomforts of the countryside. Running hot water and heating had become a necessity. I felt sorry for the Shackletons, Mrs Stringer's uncle and aunt, who had to get up at the crack of dawn and feed their chickens and constantly replace the water that had frozen in the trough. I also found Mrs Stringer's taste in music and art tedious; I had outgrown her as my education had widened my horizons.

Swineshead was only a short bus trip away, and I went to visit the Manfields for a few days. It was just like old times. I helped with the churning of the butter and other chores, and had endless teas at the homes I visited in the village. Even John started – at first tentatively – to tease me as before. In the evenings I sat by the fire with my knitting, only now it was a sweater for Frank. Wherever I turned, I found samples of my handiwork: cushion covers, chairbacks and tablerunners I had embroidered, and of course the hotwater bottle covers I crocheted. Mrs Manfield was wearing a sweater and cardigan which I had knitted.

I read in the newspaper that another 500 GI brides were being shipped to America the first week in March. The waiting became quite unbearable. I was informed by the US authorities that I could take 200 lbs of baggage, which seemed quite ridiculous. I never had that much. They expected to send my movement orders within a month. I started to count the days.

On March 6 I wrote to Frank:

> ... I miss you more than words can say and I only live for the day when we'll meet again. I miss just the whole of you from the tips of your sweet curls, five inches above your head, to the tips of those beautiful boots which I have so often felt during a dance. I miss those two deep lines by the side of your mouth which nearly reach your ears when you grin. I miss your snoring at night and your indifference at my frequent outbursts. Above all, I miss those lovely arguments when our fat heads clashed and how nice it was to make up again . . .

I could no longer spend time at other people's houses. Time hung heavy on my hands and I felt the need to occupy myself with something that would make the time pass quicker. Connie suggested that I stay with her brother and sister-in-law in Welwyn Garden City. They had three little boys and could use some help. Besides I would be close to London, in case I was called to the American offices. I took a bus to see them straightaway.

I liked Henry and Martha, and the house was pleasant and bright. I would be a mother's helper in return for my keep. I did not receive any pocket money, but at least it was a 'temporary' permanent address. Connie had been afraid that I would not warm to Martha as she was German-born with the characteristics ascribed to German *Hausfrauen*, humourless, extremely clean and well-organized. Above all, Martha was very thrifty. Henry was an engineer with the railways. I liked him better than Martha although he was quiet and morose. I did not find out the reason why until much later, when Connie told me that he had been viciously accused of treason because he had been a frequent visitor to Germany before the war, was fond of everything German and had taken a German wife. He was forced to stand trial on these trumped up charges but was vindicated. The ordeal took its toll.

The three little boys: John (five), Andrew (two), and Henry (nine months), were very cute and I grew very fond of them. I wrote to Frank that I was gaining experience coping with little kids.

Henry housed a huge collection of records (78s) in his library. He traded regularly and had the most up-to-date selection of classics. I made it my job to programme a number of works which we would listen to that evening when the little ones were in bed. From time to time, I took the train to London to queue up at the American Embassy in Grosvenor Square. There was no way to rush things.

Frank had moved back with his mother and sister Celina in Philadelphia. They lived in a small walk-up apartment in the Olney area of the city. Both women worked. His mother sewed corsets and brassières for her sister, Rosalie, who had preceded her to America and ran a successful business in the centre of the city. She not only employed Frank's mother, Anna, but also her brother, Wolf, who was the accountant for the store. She also offered Celina a job as a saleslady, but Celina soon tired of being treated less favourably than the other girls who worked there. She left to make a successful career as a fitter of foundation garments at Blauner's, a large department store in Philadelphia.

Anna did not earn very much, although she was very skilful, but she was glad to be close to her sister and brother and to support her little family. Her passions were food shopping and cooking. She picked and chose the produce very carefully, to the shopkeepers' annoyance, and she only bought 'the best'. It gave her pleasure to feed her family and visitors.

By this time, Frank's family was reconciled to the idea of his marriage. At least I was Jewish! He sang my praises to them and described my attributes in glowing terms. They busily prepared for my arrival. A new refrigerator was bought, a pull-out studio couch installed in the living-room, a coffee table was added and lots of knick-knacks that my sister-in-law was so fond of. Shoes and bags were shoved under the double bed where my mother and sister-in-law slept, to make room for my belongings. Frank and I were delegated to the studio couch in the living-room, not the best arrangement, but the only feasible one. Both mother and Celina wrote to me and also sent packages of clothing and canned food. They also included nylon stockings, a very desirable item at the time. Girls gave anything for nylons! In order to avoid paying import duty for this treasure, they carefully concealed them between the pages of magazines.

Frank wrote to me suggesting that we should have a Jewish wedding ceremony at his aunt's house, officiated by Rabbi Aaron Decter, an army chaplain whom we met briefly in Cardiff and a friend of the family. It would be advantageous, he thought, for the whole family to meet me, and of course there would be presents.

Finally, at the end of April 1946, my papers came through and I was told where and when to report on May 1st.

> Everything is ready [I wrote], my trunk is at the station. It only weighs 140 pounds.
>
> Saying goodbye to Günter was not as easy as I thought. After all he is all I have of my own flesh and blood and that has drawn us closely together. I shall never forget all he has done for me in the past . . . I have

so much to say to you that I hope I don't burst in mid-ocean.

Have decided to write an article on the adventures of a G.I. Bride and may start it on the trip. Stand on the Statue of Liberty and wave the big hankie I made. I'll spot you!

I took the train to London and from there to Salisbury, and eventually arrived at Tidworth Barracks to join the 100 or so war brides assembled there. Two more letters followed in which I complained about the 'ugly, common' girls the Yanks had married. I felt lonely and lost in this crowd; they were not my type of friends.

This sprawling camp was built on Salisbury Plain not far from Stonehenge and the charming town of Salisbury with its towering cathedral. Most American soldiers who came to England had passed through this complex of low, wooden huts. Frank was stationed there before being shipped to France in 1944. Now it was used for the many British war brides who were allowed free passage to America, courtesy of the Government.

We had to stay several days at the camp in order to be processed by American officers and checked out by a medical team. The girls spent their time viewing movies, playing cards and exchanging stories, not always clean ones! I visited Salisbury for one day with a group of them.

German prisoners of war, who manned the kitchen, served us our meals. I told Frank how I felt about that in the last of the 40 letters I had written while we were separated:

> These P.W.s all around get on my nerves. You should hear the remarks they make about the girls! I'm glad they don't understand them. These Germans certainly look everyone up and down. I often feel like turning around and swearing at them, but then I don't want to give myself away.

They must have been trained to cook for American tastes, because who, in England, would serve bacon and sausage along with pancakes swimming in syrup?

The girls who had married GIs came from different backgrounds. Most of them were working girls with little education, who expected to find the easy life in America. I am sure many were disappointed when they finally met their 'Yanks' on their home turf. Of this particular group, 90 per cent were going to the South and Mid-West to join their husbands. I only met one girl who was bound for New York. She was a teacher from Liverpool. I decided to overlook the fact that she was a spiritualist. At least she was more educated and interesting than the rest and we became friendly. I was the only Jewish girl in the group!

Finally we were transferred to Southampton. When I glimpsed the ocean liner that was to carry the war brides to America, I sensed there was something very familiar about this ship. Could it be? . . . Yes, it *was* the *SS Washington*! What a coincidence! It was only fitting that the same liner should now take me to another continent. England had been just a stop on the way that had stretched into an eight-year stay. I was leaving my teens behind. My worn but serviceable, brown suitcase with my few belongings was accompanying me. I was a married woman, ready to establish a home for Frank and myself in a new country, in another world.

8 • The Past Revisited

America became my home. Frank and I worked, studied, and lived on very little money. Frank attended college under the GI Bill and started to teach in the Philadelphia school system. I worked at the main branch of the Free Library until a month or so before the birth of our son, Julian, in November, 1947. A daughter, Nina, followed two and a half years later. We had bought a house in Camden, New Jersey. By the time Julian was attending the Jewish Nursery School, I became interested in pre-school education and started to substitute on a regular basis. I took courses at a New Jersey college and eventually entered the field of nursery school education. Frank continued his graduate studies earning a Ph.D. which enabled him to teach at area universities.

Günter and Connie had also enlarged their family in the meantime. They now had two boys, Peter and Laurence, and much later, a girl, Fiona. Günter had gone back to work in the textile industry for a company that dealt in woven labels.

My correspondence with England was frequent – not only with Günter, but I wrote to the Manfields, Mrs Stringer-Jones, Daintree, and friends from school and from Cardiff.

In 1960 I received a sum of money from the German government as *Wiedergutmachung* (restitution) for loss of education and a share of the value of the property my parents had owned. I did not want the money. On the other hand, it would have been foolish to refuse and maybe it could best be spent on something pleasurable. We decided to take the children – then ten and twelve – to Europe.

Günter and his younger son, Laurence, met us in Paris,

bringing with them a tiny Morris Mini-Minor car which he had bought at our request. After Frank got the hang of driving this overgrown baby-carriage – or pregnant roller skates, as the children dubbed it – we loaded our suitcases on top, our kids in the back and drove through Belgium and Holland via Germany to Denmark. Lübeck was the first sizeable German city that we visited. I had dreaded staying in Germany. As hard as I tried, the harsh sound of the language turned me off. I scanned the faces of older people especially. They were my parents' generation. Where were they when the Jews were being persecuted and deported, sent to camps and gassed? The extermination camps were not located so far from the cities. When a policeman harshly ordered us to move ahead, I froze. 'Let's get out of here,' I implored my husband.

We continued on to Denmark. Along the way we stopped at historical places, museums, and churches. Passing through the peaceful Danish countryside, Nina fed every horse with sugar cubes pilfered from every restaurant that had them. The children climbed all the church towers en route and we visited Hans Christian Andersen's house. In Ribe, we pointed out to them storks which had nested on wheels placed on chimneys.

Together with our 'Mini', we boarded a ferry boat to England to stay with Günter and Connie for a couple of weeks. They had built a lovely house in Northwood, outside London. While there, we took a short trip to Cardiff to visit Daintree Duke, who was now retired from the library. She was very pleased to meet my family.

Besides visiting Cardiff, we drove to Swineshead. I wanted to prove to Frank and the children that there really was such a place. We parked at the post-office. Mrs Nicholson, greeted me warmly as did her oldest daughter, Edna. Not much had changed in the village, except that now there was electricity and running water. 'Kosycott' had burned down, the thatched roof having caught fire. The Manfields had moved to a nearby town in Buckinghamshire, where John had settled after

143

23 Visiting the Manfields, 1960

getting married. Harold was married, too, and lived on the Isle of Wight. I took my family to see Mary and 'My Ducky'. Both had aged greatly but were delighted to make a lavish lunch for us. For the next ten years we corresponded. Mary kept me informed about her family. They celebrated their golden wedding anniversary in 1970. Uncle Jim died a few years later, close to 90 years old. John's wife wrote to me a short while afterwards that Aunt Mary had passed away, too.

Subsequently there were many more flights to England to see the family, although we didn't take the children anymore. On one occasion I met Mrs Stringer in Bedford with her new husband. We had very little to talk about. Our lives were so different now. I still continued to write to her at Christmastime until her letters ceased and I could only assume that she had died. She had no family who could have informed me.

In 1979, Frank and I went on an extended trip to Israel, Greece, Italy, and England with the intention of stopping in Berlin for a few days. Frank had been urging me to go back, to make my peace with the past. Besides, I had been corresponding with Dorit again and wanted to see her.

Dorit had been evacuated to the Saarland in 1943, as she told me later, where she continued her education and earned a teaching degree. When the war was over, she went back to a destroyed Berlin. Almost ten years later, in 1952, Dorit took her school vacation in England in order to improve her English. With the intention of trying to find me, she turned to the Jewish Committee located in Bloomsbury House in London and was directed to a Miss Freund. As soon as she mentioned my name and, much to her surprise, this lady not only knew me but told Dorit that she had rented a room from my parents before coming to England. She advised Dorit not to write to me directly but to let her contact me first, as I may not be interested in writing to a German. Of course, I wrote to her. When Dorit told me what Miss Freund had said, I was horrified.

'But didn't you object?' I asked.

'No', she answered, 'I felt that it was quite possible that you did not want to be in touch with me again.'

Dorit was teaching English and Psychology at a high school. She was a strong believer in introducing her students to the infamous history of the Nazis. Her parents had both died. She had never married and lived in a small apartment with her three cats.

Our first meeting was strained. My first visit back to my home town filled me with contradictory feelings. The Berlin Wall was in place, and we took a guided tour into the Communist sector. Our driver was jovial, with a thick Berlin brogue which amused very few passengers, since most of them were foreign tourists. The tour was grim. At the checkpoint, a Russian guide boarded the bus. We were not allowed to bring any magazines with us and our passports were carefully scanned. Shabbily dressed people scurried around, loaded down with shopping baskets. The houses, especially apartments, looked drab and dull. Their sameness tired the eyes. All community facilities were pointed out to impress on us how well the Communist regime took care of its people. The only stop was at a massive, ugly monument erected to the glory of the Russian Soldier. There we were allowed to stretch our legs, use the facilities, and buy some bad-tasting refreshments before going back to the brighter and more affluent Western Sector.

Günter and Connie met us in Berlin, and it took the edge off my discomfort. He had made the trip a few times, once especially to see a German couple who had written to him that they had some of our parents' property in their possession. It had been left with them for safekeeping. Günter had picked up from them a set of German silver cutlery, a service for 12, a few pieces of jewellery, and – as if by a miracle – the enamelled brooch which my ancestor wore pinned to her lace collar on that portrait in our library.

In the years that followed, Günter and Connie visited us in America, as did Dorit and my two nephews, Peter and Laurence. Günter had gone into business for himself in London, supplying woven labels to many prestigious clothing manufacturers. Eventually, he bought a flat in London close to Regent's Park and within walking distance of his office.

This little office, a third floor walk-up just off Oxford Circus, became a 'salon' where Günter entertained his friends for sumptuous lunches. The small refrigerator in the tiny kitchen was packed with patés and smoked fish from Marks and Spencer's, and the kettle was constantly boiling for tea.

Unfortunately, Günter had been diagnosed as diabetic and had to adhere to a strict diet, not at all to his liking. In January, 1984, he suffered heart failure, and – after being in a coma for almost three weeks – he died. The day of his death, I was taking a shower, and my thoughts were concentrated on him. I felt his presence. In my mind I formulated a letter to his children to let them know what he had done for me, how he had taken the job of parenting so seriously, and how much he meant to me. A few hours later, Connie called with the sad news. That was the closest I have ever come to a spiritual experience.

My daughter Nina and I flew to London for the funeral. Günter had requested cremation and a non-denominational service. Connie was hard put to find someone to preach the eulogy. His good friend, Hans, suggested asking the sexton of his synagogue, whom both Connie and Günter had met at his house previously. This man said the *Kaddish* (prayer for the dead) for my brother, which comforted me.

After Günter's death, I had no desire to visit London again. He had been for me the life-force in the city, chauffeuring us around, purchasing theatre tickets, setting up dinner parties at the flat, or making reservations at out-of-town restaurants.

In June of 1989, I saw notices about the reunion of the *Kindertransport* in the local Jewish papers. It was to take place in Harrow, near London. I decided to attend. Frank wanted to accompany me, and we arranged to stay with Günter's now married daughter, Fiona, who lived with husband Bob not far from London.

June 20 was the hottest day in England since the summer of 1976, but the people lining up outside the entrance to the large hall of the Harrow Leisure Centre did not seem to mind. Anticipation was running high. Who were they going to meet, was it going to be joyful or painful, what memories would be jogged by this confrontation with the past?

Individuals were walking up and down the long line of elderly people, anxiously scanning faces, trying to find one of the *Kinder* they knew 50 years ago. In the crowd, I spotted the two people I had met in Philadelphia before this event: Herbert Heineman and Gertrude Baron, and we waited together to have our tickets scrutinized at the narrow entrance. Security was tight. Once inside, there were over 100 tables, each one bearing the name of a city, most of them in Germany. Vienna also had many tables, as did Berlin. A few bore Czech names. Ten thousand of us had come from these cities after the fateful *Kristallnacht*, before the declaration of the Second World War in September 1939. By a miracle we had survived, we had escaped the Holocaust that had taken the lives of our parents and families. From many of the speakers on the podium we learned that a few courageous women had set this programme in motion by badgering the Home Secretary and other officials of the British government, by begging Lords and philanthropists to finance the venture. One Dutch Christian woman even pleaded with Adolf Eichmann personally to release 500 children to her care. These children, mostly between the ages of 10–15 – although some were much younger – were gathered up in Berlin, Breslau, Frankfurt, Vienna, Prague, etc., tagged and labelled and loaded onto trains, ocean liners and ferries in groups of 100–200.

They had spent their time in England either in British families, hostels or boarding schools, scattered all over the country. The majority of *Kinder* had made their home in Great Britain, accepted British nationality, married and raised families in the country that gave them refuge. About one-third were eventually reunited with their parents. The reunion rekindled memories of their past. If they were lucky, they found some who had shared the same residence or school.

After a Memorial Service conducted by Rabbi Dr. Isaac Levy and assistant rabbis, several dignitaries from the Government and representatives of the British Jewry welcomed the 1,000 who were gathered at Harrow. Not least of the speakers was Mrs Bertha Leverton, herself a former *Kind*, who was responsible for organizing this reunion and so successfully executed this tremendous undertaking. Many of us had corresponded with her prior to June and to us she was 'Bertha'. The applause that greeted her was proof of our appreciation.

Our meals had been prepaid and were served on a covered tray which had to be collected from a designated station. Long queues formed at lunchtime. No matter, you scrutinized your neighbour's name-tag which stated the present name, former name, and place of origin. You talked, you socialized, you made new friends. People milled around looking for someone from their home-town, someone from the same hostel or school, or anyone with whom they had shared experiences. At the back of the room the walls were covered with large photographs of the arrival of the *Kinder*, and people were scanning them looking for themselves or somebody they knew. One crippled man in his late sixties, joyfully pointed to a kid with a large cap, telling every passerby, 'That's me, that's me.' On the far side of the room a table had been set up selling books written by former *Kinder* about their lives, and at another table there were mementos for sale. Also a large bulletin board was put up, which was soon covered with messages, some including pictures.

The souvenir brochure listed the *Kinder* who had purchased tickets for the reunion. Many were busily scanning the pages for names of friends and acquaintances. Those who had changed their names to more English-sounding ones, and many of the girls who had married, had their original names in brackets to help identification. Then there were those living in Israel who had chosen Israeli names, and yet others with the well-known Jewish names. How would you know that a Paul Cohen from Hamburg was the boy you once knew?

By the afternoon, not only had the heat risen in this hall without air conditioning, but so had the fever of excitement. People were hugging and kissing, crying and laughing. It was no wonder that the speakers who addressed the crowd from the platform constantly had to ask for quiet and cooperation.

After an ample and tasty evening meal, a concert was presented which included a pianist, a percussionist, a choral group, and finally the talented old-timer, Larry Adler and his harmonica.

The second day was less well-attended, as there was a transport strike in England and the Underground and most buses were not running. Some people were also obligated to return to their jobs. For me, it proved more exciting than the first day, since all tables were marked with the name of a hostel or school, and I soon spotted the table marked: Bunce Court School. It was thrilling to find at least a dozen people who shared the same experiences! I recognized an old boy friend and a few other schoolmates, but some faces and names I could not recall, although they remembered me. None of us had forgotten our outstanding headmistress, Anna Essinger. We reminisced about teachers, staff, and fellow students. The more we talked, the more we remembered. Memory is a strange phenomenon, tucked away in the back of the brain, some of it is vivid, and some buried and vague; but when jogged by occasions, events, or places, it comes to life and people are visualized. It is an exhilarating experience. But we do have the power to deny memory when it is painful to recollect. I met one girl who had been at school and had come to the reunion from Brazil. She claimed to have no recollections of her school years. She only remembered that she was disliked and unhappy.

People had a hard time concentrating on the many speakers who came up to the microphone to relate their experiences, and the reminders to the *Kinder* to keep quiet and give them full attention, were numerous. One woman talked of her loneliness and yearning for love, another about the acceptance by a British gentile family who adopted her and the cruelties of the natural children in the household. Some told of being sent out to work at the age of 14, of losing their identity and of their treatment as enemy aliens by the country that had rescued them from the same enemy. The stories were not new to us. We all had a story, some happy, some sad, but every one of us applauded the country and the people who had opened their doors and assured our survival. In the evening there was another concert, this one by the talented musicians amongst the *Kinder*.

Energies were spent, the transport strike made many anxious to depart early. We said our goodbyes, vowing to keep in touch. The reunion had been a great success; we had been children again. We had recaptured just a piece of our childhood which the Nazi regime had denied us.

A short time after the London trip, I was surprised to receive a lengthy letter from Steven Mendelsson. He had been at the *Kindertransport* reunion, and after reading through the list of people in attendance, had found my name. A pity that we had not discovered this earlier. We could have met! His life had been eventful. He had been active in Jewish Youth groups in London while being apprenticed to a toolmaker. After working in the south of London creating several Habonim groups, he was recruited in 1947–48 by the Israeli Government for *Aliya Beth*, an illegal immigration operation. Steven was secretly sent to France where he escorted hundreds of concentration camp survivors from DP camps in Germany to the south of France. They travelled to the coastal regions under cover of night, almost all the way on foot. There they were picked up and taken to Palestine.

After this mission, Steven went back to England and joined a Hachshara (training farm). After a year, he emigrated to Israel where he enlisted in the army and spent three and a half years. Due to his knowledge of toolmaking, he was put in charge of making weapons and ammunition. This military workshop later became the Israeli Armaments Industries. He divided his time between the workshop and active duty as an Infantry Commander.

Eventually, Steven returned to England and completed his formal studies at night and weekends while holding a job to support himself. He met his South African wife in England while she was on a tour of Europe, and they are happily married with three grown children. After various jobs in management consulting which took him to Sweden, America, and Germany, he settled in the steel capital of Britain, Sheffield. At present he lectures at the University as well as the Polytechnic College, writes newsletters, and does consulting for local industry.

Steven and his wife are observant Jews, active in the Synagogue. He credits me with having changed his whole approach to life. At the time when we met at Churton Camp, he had turned away from all things Jewish, feeling that this part of his life should be forgotten. By chance a friend suggested going to the Habonim camp in the countryside, away from the noise and hubbub of the machine shop where they worked. Not only did he meet me then, but he made fast friendships with the people in charge who were very much immersed in Zionism with the definite aim of reclaiming Palestine for the Jews.

I hardly think that I was the main force that propelled Steven to service in the fight for Israel. At that time, he was open to other influences, but it is flattering to think that he always considered me one of the main inspirations. We have been writing to each other regularly and met at his home in Sheffield in the summer of 1993.

In 1990 Frank and I decided to take a trip to eastern Europe. The Berlin Wall had been demolished six months earlier. We would be able to travel freely, see Dorit again, and visit many of my childhood haunts. By now, I had a desire to be at peace with my past.

This journey was very different from my first visit 11 years earlier. The city was whole again and in parts unrecognizable to me. The house where I had lived had either been bombed or demolished, for in its place stood a more modern apartment house. Only an old iron pump still exists on the corner of Pestalozzistrasse, where it has been standing as far back as I can remember.

Dorit was only too happy to accompany us on our various excursions. One of them took us across the vast Potsdamer Platz where the wall once stood, into the Eastern sector with its solid traffic jams and endless red lights, to the old Jewish cemetery of Weissensee. For inexplicable reasons, the Nazis had preserved it and we found it overgrown but otherwise well marked and the tombstones in good condition. Many famous Jews are buried there, musicians, artists, writers, and businessmen. We recognized many of the names. In the small office, I inquired about my grandmother's grave. The records were well preserved, and I was told that not only my grandmother, Balbina Jachmann, but also her husband, Simon – who had died in 1909 – were buried there. We were handed a little map with the location of the stones marked. Both gravestones were well preserved and readable. I had touched the past. I had established contact with my family.

The three of us also visited the solid red schoolhouse Dorit and I attended as well as my Jewish secondary school in the Eastern sector. The building is now used as a vocational school, but the Hebrew inscription is still visible over the door, and a plaque has been affixed to the wall to commemorate the philosopher Moses Mendelssohn, whose grave is in a small cemetery adjacent to the school. His bust had adorned the top of the tomb in the days when I went to school there. It had been destroyed, but a gravestone was erected in his memory in the former cemetery which now served as a park.

Only a short block away on the Oranienburgerstrasse stands the proud New Synagogue, its Moorish dome towering over the rather modest and narrow houses of the neighbourhood. It had been partially destroyed on *Kristallnacht*, and bombings had taken their toll of the remaining structure.

At present, it is being restored and will serve as the central place of worship for all Berlin Jews. This building used to house a museum. It was there that the portraits of my ancestors had been exhibited in the late thirties. I recall visiting the museum to see their familiar faces in a different setting. I was hoping to trace them through this Synagogue.

One of the *Kinder*, whom I had met at the reunion and who lived in Berlin, gave me the name of Dr Hermann Simon, the Director of the congregation. I managed to arrange a meeting with him the day before leaving the city. He was intrigued by my story. Yes, he had some exhibit catalogues in his possession which had survived the destruction of the Synagogue. They had even unearthed the original *Ner Tamid* (Eternal Light) which dated from 1866. He promised to look through his materials and would call me the next morning. Anxiously we awaited his call before setting out for Prague.

Dr Simon kept his word. He had found the catalogue of the exhibit dated November 1936 titled *Unsere Ahnen* (Our Ancestors). The portraits were of Röschen and Aron Mendel Jacobi. She had died in 1881, her husband in 1864 in Posen. The owner was listed as great-grandson Eugen Lehmann. The artist was not identified. Dr Simon had also located a community newsletter of November of that year, which had reproduced Aron Mendel's picture. The photograph was credited to Herbert Sonnenfeld, a prominent photographer. It just so happened, Dr Simon informed me, that there was an exhibit of his work at the Berlin Museum which portrayed Jewish life in Berlin before the war.

We delayed our departure, waiting for Dr Simon to send us photocopies of his findings by special messenger. He was anxious for me to have all the information in my possession. He also suggested that I get in touch with the photographer's widow, Leni, who resided in New York. She was also a photographer.

I called her on my return home. We talked about Berlin and

24 Deserted Street in Theresienstadt

her late husband's show, the opening of which she had attended. She still had strong feelings about Germany and had been very unhappy and uncomfortable on returning there. She had little hope of recovering the photograph or negative in question but she would look for it and let me know. When she and her late husband left in 1939, they took a very limited selection of their work.

I did not hear from her. I had to be satisfied with the knowledge I had gained. At least I know that the brooch in my possession belonged to my great-great-grandmother Röschen. I wondered about the paintings. Were they destroyed? Or are they hanging in some small museum or possibly in someone's home? I possess the brooch as proof of ownership, but someone could have bought the pictures in good faith. Maybe my parents were forced to sell them when their circumstances changed so drastically? In my fantasy, I see them on a living-room wall or on display in a prestigious art gallery, and I

155

would walk up to them and pull the brooch out of its box. 'They're mine,' I would say, 'Look, I have the brooch this lady is wearing. I am her great-great-granddaughter.'

Our next stop was Theresienstadt. Only 30 miles north of Prague, it was directly on the way. We drove comfortably in a rented car, and my thoughts flew back to 1943, when my parents and many other Jews made this trip in a crowded railway car. In 1941, this small community of about 7,000 inhabitants had been commandeered by the Nazis. All residents were expelled, and barbed wire was strung around the area creating a ghetto for Jews deported from Czechoslovakia, Germany, Austria, Holland, Denmark, and later Slovakia and Hungary.

The signposts directed us to Terezin, the Czech name of the town, and we dutifully turned off the main highway at the arrow. Was this the place? This dead-looking village, deserted, unfriendly, bleak, and shabby? Where were the people who lived here? Why did no one venture out on this gloriously warm and sunny day? Was this a ghost town? But wait, there must be people living behind these closed windows. I saw curtains and flower pots and then noticed a few people furtively hiding in the shadows and a lonely worker pushing a cart down the street. Were they afraid to show their faces? Didn't they feel the presence of the more than 140,000 souls who had passed through this place, where misery and deprivation had killed more than 84,000, where every stone was witness to people's suffering?

The street called *Dlouga* was formerly *Lange Strasse* (Long Street), where my parents had lived. I could not locate the house number, but that may have changed. On the corners of houses we discovered the faint markings 'Block' followed by numbers. Why had nobody erased these signs of the Nazis?

I looked up at the narrow windows and imagined my mother's face. I would have shared her fate if I had not been sent to England. I would have joined the children's art class, which was organized by Friedel Dicker-Brandeis, an art educator who guided those under the age of 14 to express their innermost feelings on paper with crayons and paint.

Many of the artistic creations survived, and selections were displayed in Prague at the Alt-Neu Synagogue, upstairs in two crowded rooms. They were divided into three categories: life at camp, recollections of home, and imaginary subjects. Every picture was signed, and a card cited the name and age of the creator. I used to be good at art. Would my pictures have been displayed? Would my name have been augmented with the Czech feminine ending of *ova*, which gave such a strange sound to the many German names?

A photograph of the inspired teacher also was prominently displayed. Of the 15,000 children who passed through Theresienstadt, barely 100 survived. Their artistic output stands as a monument to their spirit.

Many well-known artists, writers, poets, musicians, and composers had spent time in Theresienstadt. Most of them lost their lives, many because they dared to portray the misery of their existence and the cruelty of the Nazis.

However, the world is in possession of much of their creative work that miraculously survived – artwork, plays, poems, writings and music, much of it smuggled out of the ghetto at great risk. Many talented teachers and educators also taught academic subjects to the children in secret, since the Nazis did not allow the children to be educated. Their objective was to groom them for slave labour.

We followed the former Long Street to a small clearing where a section of railway track came out of nowhere, the two rail lines crossing – the end of the line. Behind the tracks was a brick wall with a memorial plaque.

The plaque showed a group of people – a mother, father, children, and other relatives – stumbling forward into the unknown. The faces did not look like Jewish faces, and if it had not been for a Hebrew sign around the neck of the young

157

boy, I would not have known this was a memorial to Jews. The adjoining panel showed a weeping willow tree.

We continued down the road, looking for the cemetery where my father must have been buried, since he had died here in early 1944. As though by chance, we came upon two grottoes, enclosed behind iron railings. One contained a large *Magen David* in the background, and several candelabras were placed around the space. The other held a tall single candle-holder and a wooden carriage placed in front of a large cross.

Later, we read that these ceremonial halls were built by the Nazis in anticipation of a visit by the Red Cross in 1945 – right before the end of the war – in order to prove that this was a model camp that provided 'halls of mourning' – one for Jews and one for those of Jewish ancestry who had been raised in the Christian faith. A film had even been made portraying the life at Theresienstadt as a pleasant vacation resort for Jews, where people were entertained by music and theatre perfor-mances and lived a life of leisure. The title of this shameful film was: *Der Führer schenkt den Juden eine Stadt* (The Führer presents the Jews with a town).

But where was the cemetery? Finally, we found the turnoff that directed us to the *Krematorium*. A parking lot, empty except for one other car, indicated we had reached our desti-nation. A pebbled walk led to a field of identical gravestones, dominated by a large, solid stone menorah. The stones bore no names, just numbers and a *Magen David*.

Would anyone be able to tell me which stone marked my father's resting place? No, the old man in the adjacent build-ing informed us, all records were kept in Prague. He only presided over a small exhibit of children's art, a few dolls carefully constructed out of scraps of cloth, leather and wool, dressed in tiny hand-knitted sweaters and socks. The exhibit also included glass cases, which held identity cards, food vouchers, SS orders, photographs of prisoners and other memorabilia of people who had once been confined there.

Behind the exhibition room were the ovens of the crematorium and standing before them, the conveyors on wheels that had guided the bodies into the fire. I could look no further.

We bought several books about Theresienstadt, beautifully illustrated with many coloured photographs and reproductions of paintings and drawings. In silence we made our way back to the parking lot. The other car had already left. Without speaking, we sat in our comfortable *Opel*, sorting out our impressions. It was time to go on to Prague. I noticed a dustbin nearby and decided to get rid of some accumulated debris. Surprisingly, the bin contained discarded boxes of meatballs and bags of bread. What would the starving inmates of this place have given for all this food?

We were deeply absorbed in our thoughts as we drove towards Prague. A short distance down the road stood the Terezin fortress. Constructed between 1780 and 1791, it was known as the 'Little Fortress.' It was utilized as barracks and later as a jail for soldiers and dissidents. In 1914, prisoners of war from Russia, Serbia, and Italy were interned there. Not until 1939, when the Germans occupied Czechoslovakia, was the fortress used to imprison anti-Fascist fighters. It became a police prison of the Gestapo and later a concentration camp for freedom fighters. More than 32,000 prisoners passed through its gates.

Jews were a special group sent here for violating orders, often trivial orders. Of the many who lived here, thousands died due to lack of food, disease, torture, and random executions. We walked up to the black-and-white-outlined entrance but were not in the mood to view the museum on the premises.

A few days later in Prague, in a dark building that housed a kosher restaurant downstairs, on the same street as the Alt-Neu Synagogue, I looked for the records from Theresienstadt. I was directed to an office upstairs. The door was marked 'Evidence.' This room held 140,000 lives, packed together in card files, as crowded as they once had lived. A helpful little lady asked for my parents' names and without much trouble pulled two cards from the filing cabinet. She made a Xerox copy of these cards, which carefully noted the name, birthdate, their number, the date of my father's cremation, and the number of my mother's deportation transport. The road ended here.

We continued our travels via Budapest and Vienna to Amberg, a small town in Bavaria – a stone's throw from the Czech border. It is here that my only surviving cousin, Karla, had settled with Paul. Argentina had proven to be no longer a safe haven for them and their son Pedro felt that he could build a better future for his wife and son in Europe. A dentist by profession, he found it advantageous to practise in Germany under their socialized health plan. He had been raised speaking German in his home, so the language posed no problem. His wife, Lucrecia, is of Italian–Argentinian origin and Pedro translated everything into Spanish for her, until her knowledge of German was adequate. Their son, Federico, born in Germany grew up bilingual. They like their lives in this picturesque little town nestling in the hills of Bavaria. Karla and Paul, or Poly – as he calls himself – live in an apartment nearby, happy to be close to their loved ones in their advancing years. I asked Karla numerous questions about the family, and she shared many of the photographs she had by duplicating them for me.

At the *Kindertransport* reunion I had met one of my former schoolmates from Bunce Court, Martin Lubowski, who is working on collecting archives of the school which are to be deposited in the Wiener Library in London. I promised to help him by supplying some of my own photographs and documents. In turn, he could give me addresses of former students and a history of the school. Prior to our trip, Martin informed me of a historical event which was to take place in Ulm, Anna Essinger's birthplace. The local High School *Gymnasium und*

25 In Front of Anna Essinger's Portrait

Realschule was going to change its name to honour her memory. There was to be a celebration, all alumni and friends were most welcome. We adjusted our travel dates to include this happening and drove there from Amberg. It was a beautiful September day, warm and sunny. The Bavarian landscape was green and lush. We arrived in time to join a large crowd composed mostly of students of all ages, who were occupying rows and rows of seats in an amphitheatre in front of the school entrance. A large reproduction of Anna Essinger's photographic portrait hung on one side of the stage. Frank and I squatted on some steps and waited for the show to begin.

The older students had prepared a series of skits which recalled scenes from T.A.'s life and teachings. With song and dance the students showed us a repressed classroom atmosphere which changed dramatically with the entry of an innovative teacher, the opening of large cardboard boxes which represented the new subjects added to the curriculum, and the disdain that the authorities showed for progressive education. The most touching scene was the departure of the children from Germany when the school relocated to England. Swastika flags were hoisted in the background to show the takeover of the country by the Nazis. Teenagers dressed as parents bid their suitcase-carrying children a sad goodbye. Once in England, they sat at desks and wrote their nostalgic letters home which were read in measured phrases over the P.A. system. The show ended with fireworks and the unfurling of a large banner with 'Anna Essinger Schule' in bright red letters.

We met with others who had formerly attended her school either in Germany, Kent, or Shropshire, as I had. After viewing two films made by alumni of Bunce Court, we drove back to Amberg. I was glad to have been able to attend this event to honour a great educator who had also had a tremendous impact on my life. I had never corresponded with her while the school was in Shropshire nor after it moved back to Kent in 1946. The school closed in 1948. Anna Essinger died in 1960.

I returned home from our travels exhilarated and emotionally satisfied. So much had been revealed, so much relived, I could now delve into the past with renewed energy and greater understanding. My parents' letters which had come into my possession only a year or so earlier were a source of revelation as well as great emotion to me. Connie had delayed sending them after Günter's death, afraid of losing them in the mail. Finally she had given them to her son Peter to take to America. He, in turn, had postponed reading them, and it took a trip to California to finally take possession of them.

In November of 1990, some *Kinder* who had attended the reunion in London decided to organize a similar event in New York for those now residing in the States. Expecting about 100 responses, the organizers were overwhelmed by close to 500 applications. The meeting was moved to a hotel in the Catskill Mountains, New York State, about three hours from the city. The magic and anticipation of the London event had dissipated, at least for me and for those of us who had experienced it before. Still for many it was the first time that they were meeting their fellow *Kinder* again. Since we found ourselves at a resort hotel, the atmosphere was more relaxed, more American, with entertainment in the evenings and the usual recreational facilities available.

I met many new people as well as a few who had been at Harrow, among them two of my former schoolmates from Bunce Court. Eventually, we found 11 with the help of the computer, and we spent some time reminiscing together. Amongst the group was Michael Roemer, a film producer, who had made the classic film, *Nothing But a Man* – the first film made that depicted a black family in a role other than that of slavery or servitude. Since then he has made many documentaries and released a feature film, *The Plot Against Harry*, which dealt with Jewish family life in the fifties. Michael, though a year younger than 'our gang' at school, had been a talented and precocious youngster even then and we had included him in our plays and socials.

Bertha Leverton, the organizer of the original reunion, came over from London with a book she had edited consisting of short accounts by over 240 *Kinder*. Each one tells a different story, yet a common thread unites them – the trauma of leaving a loving secure home and being deposited in a strange country. In the course of the programme, when the *Kinder* had a chance to meet in small groups with a selected discussion leader, many hidden feelings came to light. We had lived with these emotions for close to 50 years, thinking ourselves unique in our own minds. Here was an opportunity to share our feelings with those who lived through the same experiences. We had all been victims of uprooting, abandonment and isolation and had worked hard to succeed, to find a sympathetic partner, to establish a home and to raise a family. We had made our contributions to society by qualifying for the helping professions as teachers, social workers, nurses, health technicians, and psychologists. I admired their versatility and adaptability although they were left with many emotional scars. People spoke of their fear of being left alone, a feeling of non-acceptance or open rejection, a lack of self-esteem. Most had memory blanks, especially about their farewells and train or ship journeys. I could identify with that. Several women spoke of their apprehension when parting with their children. Even sending them off to college became a traumatic experience.

Many of the *Kinder* still spoke with a heavy foreign accent, but their children were American-born and American-raised. We vowed as a group to take the responsibility of telling our children about our survival. Many young adult offspring attended this reunion and also had a chance to meet together to share their feelings.

As for myself, I felt that it was important to make contact with the *Kinder*. It helped me to sort out my own emotions and spurred me on to express myself on paper in order that my children, nephews and niece, as well as my grandchildren, may know of their heritage.

9 • Conclusion

There remained only one last mission: to visit Auschwitz.

In 1991, Frank and I travelled to Berlin again, this time as guests of the city. As one of thousands of surviving Berliners forced to leave due to Nazi persecution, I was invited by the Mayor's Office to visit Berlin at their expense. Other German cities have also issued such invitations. It was then that we decided to include Poland on our itinerary.

That year spring had been late to arrive in eastern Europe and summer was reluctant to follow. It was cold and the clouds hung heavy in the Polish sky as we drove to Oswiecim, the little town near the extermination camp just a few miles outside Cracow. The lilacs and horse chestnuts – long wilted at home – were blooming in profusion this first week in June. As the sun came out later during our journey, their candle-like blooms lit up the road like so many chandeliers.

The signposts were confusing. At every crossroad we had to make an arbitrary decision. A detour across a railway line close to our destination added to the confusion and delay, not to mention a religious procession led by gowned clergymen under a canopy preceded by a band playing hymns, that threaded its way from the church across the highway. Among them were many little girls in white frilly dresses with wreaths in their hair like miniature brides. It was Corpus Christi, an important Catholic holiday.

Finally we turned down the right road, past a military camp and parked alongside other cars and many tour buses. By this time, the sun was shining brightly. It had turned into a pleasant, warm day. Family groups, like any people on an

166

outing – with kids licking ice-cream bars – were making unguided tours around the camp.

We entered each of the barracks which contained different aspects of prison life. Most buildings bore a number, but a few were identified by their function. They contained endless cases of documents and letters mostly in German, attesting to the many commands and directives the Nazis had issued. We saw numerous lists of belongings that had been confiscated from their victims.

On the walls we noticed row upon row of portraits; faces of men and women, their names and dates of detention in Auschwitz. All were Polish names, only a few were identifiable as being of Jewish origin. The length of the women's hair varied according to the time they had stayed at the camp. On arrival they had all been shorn.

One building held large showcases of the various objects that were taken from the prisoners on arrival and stored for their possible usefulness to the Germans. There were piles of shabby and worn shoes in one case, men's, women's, even children's. How many miles had their owners been forced to walk on uneven pavements, across fields and stony paths such as the one linking the barracks? I noticed some well-worn felt slippers among the leather footwear. We also saw hundreds of eyeglasses in another enclosure, their wire rims tangled in the big pile. A sizeable showcase revealed suit-cases, leather ones brought by the affluent, cardboard ones by the poor. Each one was carefully marked in large letters by its owner. You could easily read the names. What a difficult decision it must have been to choose your most precious possessions. One had to be practical and pack only necessities for an unknown destination. Just a single suitcase was per-mitted. And how many were not even given time to make a choice?

There were also a number of baskets piled in one corner. Presumably they had contained provisions for the journey.

Another window displayed baby clothes, still another pots and pans and utensils, mostly of the enamelled variety. I was deeply affected by a large collection of braces and prostheses, wooden arms and legs, which were flung in bizarre disarray. My father had worn such a heavy, cumbersome, artificial arm. All displays – including the pile of human hair – were in climate-controlled cases to preserve them for generations to come.

We entered other buildings which contained straw pallets placed closely together. Between the crowded dormitories, small cubicles were located which housed the privileged over-seers of the barracks. He or she was at least permitted a wooden bed and chair, often a table and even a window. As in a trance, we stumbled around the rooms, often not knowing which way we had entered.

The last two buildings near the formerly electrified barbed wire with its sinister warning of skull and crossbones, had been designated for the *Sonderkommando* only. The very last one was assigned to medical experiments and sterilization of women. Nearby I caught sight of a woman visitor, with tears running down her face.

On the other side of the barbed wire stood a building surrounded by scaffolding. We recognized it as the contro-versial house of the Carmelite nuns, who had seen fit to use the facility – formerly used for storing cyanide gas – as a convent. They must have been inside, because I heard the faint sound of singsong voices in prayer coming from within. I had read that eventually this building would house a non-denominational chapel. This never came to pass. Instead, there are presently allegations that a huge monument is to be erected to 70,000 Christian victims of Auschwitz on that same property ignoring the fact that 1.5 million Jews perished there.

It was not until we entered the barracks reserved for Jewish victims that I truly felt that Auschwitz was not exclusively a memorial to Poles. A recording of prayers being recited provided a fitting background for viewing the many photographs and objects attesting to the Holocaust. Sculptures and art works depicted the suffering. Many pictures showed the martyrs and victims who gave their lives to the resistance by rising up against their oppressors and fighting in the ghettos, the sewers, in camps and hidden in the forests.

I recognized a few faces, among them Janusz Korczak, the famous doctor, author and educator who accompanied the 200 orphans from the Warsaw Ghetto to the gas chambers of Treblinka. I also spotted Vladka Meed's portrait, a fearless fighter in her youth, who survived and is now a frequent speaker at many Holocaust events. We signed the visitors' book in this building and I expressed my deep feelings.

The crematorium – the only one left standing, was the last building we visited. Next to it, were erected the gallows on which Rudolf Hoess – the infamous commander of Auschwitz – was hanged in 1947.

Frank and I left the camp drained and emotionally depleted. We lacked the strength to visit the nearby Birkenau camp. I had come to honour my mother's memory, to experience her last weeks of life but I also honoured the memory of all those who perished there. We, who were spared, must tell our children, so they in turn can tell their children what took place.

Since my memorable visit to this site of suffering and inhumanity, many Holocaust memorials have been erected including the very impressive United States Holocaust Memorial Museum in Washington, DC. It was there that I deposited my ugly brown, cardboard suitcase, the one in which I carried my heart. It deserved to be preserved for posterity. Had not a grieving mother packed it lovingly for her youngest child, her only daughter? It had crossed the Channel with the *Kindertransport*, travelled from town to town, from village to village with me, finally to cross the Atlantic Ocean, to rest in various attics and basements stuffed with cast-off clothing and outgrown baby clothes. My battered suitcase could have been amongst the many on display behind glass in Auschwitz. Their owners are no longer living, victims of atrocities, hard labour, starvation and sickness. Their memories died with them. But like me, the brown suitcase survived to bear witness. It tells of tears and hope, but more important, of being saved from the Holocaust.